Jay Conrad Levinson

W9-BOF-440

EARNING

MONEY

WITHOUT

A JOB

Revised for the '90s

An Owl Book
HENRY HOLT AND COMPANY
New York

Henry Holt and Company, Inc.
Publishers since 1866
115 West 18th Street
New York, New York 10011

Henry Holt® is a registered trademark
of Henry Holt and Company, Inc.

Copyright © 1991 by Jay Conrad Levinson
All rights reserved.
Published in Canada by Fitzhenry & Whiteside Ltd.,
195 Allstate Parkway, Markham, Ontario L3R 4T8.

Library of Congress Cataloging-in-Publication Data
Levinson, Jay Conrad.
Earning money without a job / Jay Conrad Levinson.
p. cm.
"An Owl book."
Includes bibliographical references.
1. Self-employed—Handbooks, manuals, etc.
2. Small business—Handbooks, manuals, etc.
3. Entrepreneurship—Handbooks, manuals, etc. I. Title.
HD8036.L48 1990
658.1'141—dc20 90-42942
CIP

ISBN 0-8050-1458-6 (An Owl Book: pbk.)

Henry Holt books are available for special promotions and premiums.
For details contact: Director, Special Markets.

First published in hardcover by Holt, Rinehart and Winston in 1979.

First Owl Book Edition—1991

This book was originally published by the author in substantially
different form by Prosper Press copyright © 1976.

Designed by Katy Riegel

Printed in the United States of America
All first editions are printed on acid-free paper.∞

9   10   8

OTHER BOOKS BY
JAY CONRAD LEVINSON:

Secrets of Successful Free-Lancing
The Most Important $1.00 Book Ever Written
San Francisco: An Unusual Guide to Unusual Shopping
(with John Bear and Pat Levinson)
555 Ways to Earn Extra Money
An Earthling's Guide to Satellite TV
150 Secrets of Successful Weight Loss (with Michael Lavin
and Michael Rokeach, M.D.)
Small Business Savvy
Quit Your Job!
Guerrilla Marketing
Guerrilla Marketing Attack
Guerrilla Marketing Weapons
The Ninety-Minute Hour

This book is dedicated to freedom,
and to all people who understand and affirm freedom.

Contents

Acknowledgments

First I want to express appreciation to my wife, Pat, for her constant encouragement, inspiration, enthusiasm, bright ideas, her innate quality, and most of all—her love. I also thank my gloriously iconoclastic daughter, Amy, for her energy, her faster-than-light proofreading, and her ability to spur my conscientiousness. Certainly I owe thanks to Jan Parker for helping me put this book together in the first place, to Nathan Privitt for his painstaking professionalism, and to Michael Paul Lavin for his endless information. I single out Mark Steisel for shepherding the book all the way from the inside of my head to your hands. Without question, acknowledgments are due to Michael Larsen and Elizabeth Pomada, who optimistically knew exactly what to do with the book once it was written. And finally, I wish to communicate publicly the gratitude I feel toward the late Donald Hutter of Henry Holt, who showed me the difference between a writer and an author, as well as Theresa Burns at Henry Holt, who had the wisdom to coerce me to update this book. To all the people listed above, and to the people who showed by example how to earn money without a job—thank you and bless you.

—J.C.L.

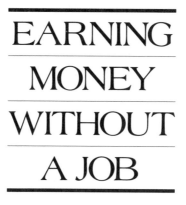

EARNING
MONEY
WITHOUT
A JOB

CHAPTER ONE

The Consciousness for the New Economics

This is a book about freedom.

This is a book about freedom from an economic system that probably has been controlling your life. In these pages is the foundation for a new system that puts *you* in control of your life. Once you have control, you will have the freedom to decide your own income, your own working hours, your own workweek, your own working conditions.

Even better, you will have enough money to expand your freedom even further. You will have the money and time to discover what you are all about, and then to be it.

Until now, to millions of people, out of a job meant out of work. But no longer. Now, you need no job to have work. You need no job to earn money. You need no job, period. In fact, once you have acted upon the information in these pages, you may never want a job again.

I have been without a job for over two decades, yet I never have been without work. I have earned considerably more money without a job than I did with a job, yet I rarely work more than three days a week. I have tasted freedom and quickly grew addicted to its pleasures. Now I wish to provide access to freedom for the rest of America. And I hope you enjoy it as much as I have.

In order to understand freedom, you must understand options, or choices. The more options you have, the more freedom you have. But many of us don't come close to realizing how many options we do have.

Psychologists tell us that if you place a rat in front of ten tunnels and place a piece of cheese at the end of one of the tunnels, the rat will find the cheese. If you then move the cheese to the end of a different tunnel, the rat still will find the cheese.

Human beings, in analogous situations, act differently. Finding the cheese missing, they don't try to look elsewhere for it. If a human being receives a paycheck and a slew of fringe benefits from a company, and suddenly they stop, he or she will not search out different tunnels. Most will try the same tunnel over and over again and rarely seek new options, much less dig a few new tunnels of their own.

But the economics of freedom suggests that there are countless tunnels: old ones, new ones, undiscovered ones, untapped ones, all readily available to you, all ready to provide a paycheck, a slew of fringe benefits, and a degree of control you may never have experienced before.

The economics of freedom deals with a lot more than economics. It deals in humanity as well, by incorporating humanity into its very essence. The economics of freedom makes money a by-product of humanity, not a central force.

To earn money without a job requires a clear understanding of your own value system. First, you've got to establish your survival values—beginning with food, shelter, clothing, utilities, medical bills, and any other costs that you deem essential. It is necessary to understand these values for two reasons: (1) to help tide you over during your first weeks or months without the security of a regular check, and (2) to help you free up as much capital as necessary for whatever methods you choose to earn money.

Next, you should establish your luxury values—vacations, boats, jewelry, frequent dining out, and anything else you have ever desired. These will enable you to set your earning goals and guide you in whatever endeavors you decide to undertake.

Understand that there is no limit to what you may crave. It is surprisingly attainable through the economics of freedom. In truth, it is what freedom implies in the first place.

At this point, it is a good idea to forget what you remember of the old economic system, the system that required you to have a job in order to survive without welfare. Instead, first look to yourself and answer basic questions.

How Many Days per Week Do You Wish to Work?

Think about it, then come up with a definite answer. Do you wish to work full or part time? The choice is yours. How many hours per day do you want to work? Which hours? It doesn't have to be an eight-hour day; it doesn't have to be nine to five.

What Income Do You Want?

This answer should be compatible with your other answers, but it still provides you with enormous choice.

I want to work three days a week, with my weekends

free. I don't care how many hours I must work as long as I can confine them to three days. I want $75,000 per year to be my income, yet I easily can survive on far less.

Ever since these have been my goals I have been able to attain and surpass them. But before I understood the economics of freedom, I didn't even know it was within my power to set my own goals.

Once you get it into your head that you have unlimited opportunities to earn money, start looking for them. You will be presented with a lot of ideas right in these pages. Remember, now you may do things you have never done before. You need not fit into your old mold. Just because you spent many years doing something doesn't mean you must still do it. Unless you want to.

Let's Be Candid

As much as I favor a life filled with freedom, I have to confess that it is not a life for everyone. I certainly cannot and do not suggest to all who ask me that they pursue the economics of freedom.

For many people, it is definitely a poor choice. These people do not or cannot have the discipline necessary for success in a life of freedom. Many of these people have the discipline, but do not have the thick skin and determination required. Others are just too separated from reality. But most people for whom the economics of freedom is contraindicated are those who enjoy receiving orders from others, who enjoy having their work assigned to them, who enjoy the security of a regular paycheck, the assertiveness of a hardheaded boss.

Many of you don't want or need the hassle of starting your own business. If that is the case, don't do it. While a large group of people will thrive with this new perception of economics, a different large group will intelligently shy away from it, realizing clearly that "this is not for me."

The economics of freedom is not a financial panacea. All it really offers is another option: an all-encompassing option. It is an alternative to life with a job, and for many, it is the next step. But for many others, it is ill advised, improper, and totally unrealistic.

I have seen friends and associates practice the economics of freedom with varied results. Most people I have observed have succeeded faster and with better results than they dreamed possible. But for others, it just plain didn't work out.

They may not have wanted freedom enough. They may have loved the theoretical concept of a life filled with freedom, but hated the reality. They may have failed to market aggressively.

Since writing my first book on the topic of working without a job, I have received many letters from people who have succeeded at it. I have received none from people who have not succeeded. Some can make it work and others cannot. You must love life enough to do the work that earns freedom.

You can be fairly accurate in predicting whether it will work for you if you can honestly describe yourself as disciplined, determined, self-motivated, and adaptive. That asks for a lot of self-knowledge.

If these words describe you, or *can* describe you, consider going for the life of a free person. If these words can in no way describe you now or in the future, perhaps you should stick to the established economic system. Self-knowledge: The more you have, the smoother your life.

■ ■ ■

Where to begin?

Check the want ads in the daily newspaper to see the jobs that are advertised. But don't consider them jobs; instead, look upon them as work that must be accomplished. Perhaps you can accomplish it without taking a job.

If you are out of a job right now, you have probably never had a better time to discover who you are, and to be that person. Try to get in touch with yourself, see what it is you want to do, and give yourself all the ego gratification you wish. Only gratify your ego the way you want, not the way some big company wants. There is a difference.

If you have no job now, you have an enormous and valuable inventory. Your inventory consists of *time.* Think of time as an asset, spend it intelligently, and realize that a standard job robs you of it. Only when you are out of a job do you have so much control over your time. So, cherish every moment, for it is even more valuable than the riches it can bring.

Like so many other aspects of human existence, earning money without a job is a combination of joys and frustrations. The frustrations come in the form of no regular paycheck, no union protection, no true security (but more than if you had a standard job), little instant success, loss of customers or clients, no lush fringe benefits, no retirement income or pensions, no clear directions from higher levels, and other frustrations that are offshoots of whatever work you select. But the joys are freedom and inner fulfillment. And I have found that they far outweigh the frustrations.

For one thing, you can eliminate the frustrations with simplicity. I once reveled in the womb of a large organization and enjoyed all the fringe benefits of the corporate structure. In fact, I enjoyed them so much that I have them back again—only this time without the corporation.

From my own income, I cover my own health insurance, life insurance, sick pay, vacation time, Christmas bonus, even retirement income. I simply decided that I needed these fringe benefits, and then I made them happen.

The economics of freedom enables you to make a decision that may be new to you: Do you wish to go it alone, or do you want to hire an organization once your income warrants it? If you are truly diligent about earning money, you will soon have enough work to rationalize taking on your own employees. But will you want to become labor-intensive? Will you want the problems of a staff? Will you be willing to put up with the complexities? Sure, a larger organization may result in a larger income, but it will eat into your freedom as well. It's a decision best made in the beginning. So as you read this book, keep it in mind. I have intentionally remained a one-man company, and I have absolutely no regrets from the decision.

At the outset, the lack of a job results in terrible insecurity. But the work that is available will give you the option to eliminate financial insecurity forever. You can choose work that results in permanent earned income—a new option for many. Or you can play for high stakes during the short haul, and accumulate enough capital to offset the lack of permanent earned income with permanent investment income. The point is, you are in control, not someone else.

Perhaps the most amazing thing about earning money without a job is how easy it is to do. The going is the toughest at the beginning. But after that, you'll wonder why you waited so long to be your own person.

For many of you, this will be your first experience with work that puts up no dead ends, sets no income limit, provides no time clock to punch, and entangles you in no red tape. It's so beautiful, it's almost scary. But you'll find such a life awfully easy to lead.

Here's the secret to the whole thing: modularity. You are not an entire system. Instead, you are part of it. You are not an entire automobile-producing company. Instead, you are a welder. You are not an entire advertising agency. Instead, you are a media buyer. You are not an entire office staff. Instead, you are a typist. You are modular—a part, but not the whole thing. And a part is all you need to be.

You have probably heard of free-lance writers and free-lance artists. The economics of freedom permits free-lance carpenters, free-lance landscapers, free-lance accountants, free-lance anything. Anything that can be done full-time can also be done part-time. Well, nearly anything.

This thinking provides economic advantages to companies and to individuals. It enables companies to accomplish the work they need to accomplish without the attendant overhead. It enables individuals to earn the money they need without the loss of freedom.

In *Future Shock,* Alvin Toffler writes of the modular corporations of the future. But the old economy has forced us into the future ahead of time. And many of us will become modular ahead of our time.

As it is for any pioneers, the first part is the hardest. Until you establish your income and work patterns, you will work the hardest. But after you have reached your economic destination, your whole life should become noticeably easier, especially your own work. So be ready to devote the most energy in the beginning, but be ready to take advantage of an abundance of ease later on. That thought alone can make the beginning easier to live with.

Because you will be modular, get to know other modular people and small modular organizations. Together, you will be able to offer the services or goods of a complete entity. Yet you will be able to maintain your own individuality. So outside service and equipment connections will prove of invaluable aid. Once you have determined a plan of action, all the allied connections to your plan can help you.

My plan of action centers around advertising. But my allied connections include marketing, film making, radio, videotape production, research, media buying, sales training, graphics, personnel, direct mail, publishing, mail order, finance, typesetting, printing, announcing, music, painting, banking, casting, photography, public relations, acting, interior design, and merchandising. Not surprisingly, most of these connections are with modular people who earn money without a job. And some of them earn a whale of a lot of money. My own income hasn't been damaged by my three additional new careers: writing books, publishing a newsletter; and speaking to groups.

Nowhere is it written that man—or woman—shall undertake one lifelong endeavor in the same field. Yet many of us remain forever in the same field. Now is the time to change, if you'd like. Nowhere is it written that people will undertake one endeavor at a time. Yet few of us are engaged in more than one income-producing effort. America in the 1800's was a time when people had one lifetime career. In the 1900's, we advanced to three jobs per lifetime. The 2000's will be a time of four or five careers, all practiced simultaneously. I suggest that you don't wait.

Become engaged in many earning endeavors, not just one. Rather than becoming a major factor in one field, consider becoming a minor factor in many fields. You now have this option.

You may work odd hours, irregular hours. You may sleep late and work till dawn. You may arise early and complete your work by noon. Though it may not have been up to you before, it certainly is all up to you now.

Become aware of the immense amount of information provided to you by the Yellow Pages. Through study of them you will learn of voids in your area, shortages, needs, and growth opportunities.

The Yellow Pages can prevent you from expending energy in overcrowded fields; the Yellow Pages can point the way to fields begging for assistance. It's all there. Let your fingers help with the earning.

Because of your newfound freedom, you can become extensions of going businesses without joining those businesses. You can become the mail-order arm of a company that doesn't yet sell by mail-order. You can become the repair department for a company that doesn't yet have a repair department (but would love to). You can become the at-home service department for service stations that never offered service at home.

Imagine a service station that picks up customers' cars after the people are asleep, fills the cars with gas, changes the oil, checks the battery, brake, and transmission fluid, makes any requested repairs, and returns the cars to the driveway or garage before the people awaken. No service station I know of offers such intelligent service. But you can become an extension of a station, and then they can offer it. That's just one of several applications of this idea.

Consider bartering. Since time is in your inventory, consider trading your time, services, or things for the time, services, or things of another. There is no necessity for money to enter into all business relationships. If you could trade a few hours a month to the phone company for free use of your telephone, it would be very similar to working a few hours a month for the money to pay the phone company. But since public utilities are probably not ready for the economics of freedom, perhaps you can effect your trade with other companies. It pays to think about it awhile.

I have enjoyed free vacations three different times by trading my writing services for plane tickets and/or rooms in hotels and condominiums. My trades were with a hotel, a condominium rental company, and a travel agency. I think we all benefited from the trades.

According to many, the ideal life would be one where your job is no different from your hobbies. And now you are offered this ideal life. If you had no need for more money, how would you spend your time? Whatever your answer, try to relate it to a money-making task. If you would like to spend your time fishing, consider becoming a fishing guide; consider running a fishing-boat charter service; consider fishing for a livelihood by selling your catch to commercial establishments.

If you would like to spend three days a week working and four days playing, you'd better know exactly what you'll do during your playtime. If you don't, you will feel less motivated to keep your workweek down to three days.

Think about all the leisure-time activities you wish to pursue, and see if some of them can be turned into profitable work. Those that can should be seriously examined as potential sources of income. Those that cannot should be enjoyed during your free time.

It is important that you definitely accomplish certain things on certain days. It is equally important that you spend certain other days accomplishing absolutely nothing. The work ethic of the old economics has led to a decline of pleasure—even during weekends. Many Americans feel that the day is wasted if nothing is accomplished.

This is nonsense. As long as you accomplish things on some days, you are entitled to accomplish nothing on other days. The economics of freedom includes personal pleasure as a guiding motivation. And freedom includes freedom from the need to accomplish.

The days that you do accomplish things must be days dedicated to earning. After a short time utilizing your earning capabilities, you will realize the difference between effort expended working and effort expended *earning*.

During your chosen workdays you should focus all your energies on earning. This means streamlining your existence and becoming as efficient an earner as possible. It means separating the games and formalities of work from the actual necessities. If you become proficient at knowing the difference, you will earn more in less time. Your work time will become far more valuable because it will translate itself into dollars. You will eliminate wasted motion and become a true earning machine. And no doubt you will be surprised at how much earning you can accomplish if that is your clear purpose.

Still, regardless of how much planning and organization you put into your life, you must always remember Murphy's Law: "Anything that can go wrong will go wrong." Merely knowing this will help when things go wrong. And you may possibly even prevent a few wrong-goings.

Remember, too, that Murphy has been described as an optimist, and many things *will* go wrong if they possibly can. You'd better be ready, intellectually and emotionally, to react. For your reactions can offset the miseries of Murphy's Law. By adapting to the disaster, you can get your energies back on track.

I have lost sources of income because of my own incompetence, the incompetence of my clients, the economy, the competition, dishonest suppliers, my wife, my lifestyle, poor results, excellent results, and for reasons I never learned. But I did learn that regardless of preparation and regardless of your own flawless behavior, things can get totally screwed up. And now that I've said it, there's not much you can do about it. That's Murphy for you.

But take heart that Murphy's Law strikes others as well. And that creates vulnerabilities and openings for you. In the course of reading this book, you will note that many of your potential sources of income already are being serviced by others. No problem—80 percent of business that is lost is due to indifference after the sale. By offering the opposite of indifference, you will appeal to the eighty customers in a hundred who might require what you have to offer. And by never appearing indifferent after you've made your own sale, you can maintain a long-term relationship with your income source. Very few divorces are requested during the honeymoon. So in all your business relationships, keep the honeymoon going for as long as possible.

The economics of freedom offers no single new way of earning money. In fact, virtually every way suggested is a way that someone is using right this moment to earn money. However, taken all together, the economics of freedom offers a whole new way of approaching life and its attendant responsibilities to earn. And this alternative is as yet invisible to the vast majority of breadwinners.

In spite of the new relationship you may develop with money, remember that it is merely a welcome accompaniment to a long life. The long life is far more valuable than the money, and once you know how to use money comfortably, you will have wealth beyond the reach of any money.

Can the economics of freedom help you to achieve a long life? The answer is *absolutely.*

A series of over a thousand interviews with one-hundred-year-old men and women, published by the Social Security Administration in Washington, D.C., revealed a fascinating pattern of living evident in most centenarians.

First of all, these extended life-spanners were self-employed. Regardless of whether they were housewives, doctors, carpenters, business proprietors, or potters, they were not beholden to anyone else.

Another factor noted was that these people worked long hours. It may be that their total involvement created an excitement and fulfillment that maintained health while retarding the aging process.

Third, the hundred-year-olds were serene. Serenity must have come from enjoyment of life, from a deep faith, from a keen sense of reality, and from the ability to be insulated from the hard knocks that certainly are a part of life. I wonder if they got smarter as they got older. I think that is true of me. I believe that is the bonus that comes with age.

A fourth factor shared by the centenarians was moderation. Certainly that is an important part of the economics of freedom. If you have enough freedom, you are not forced to immoderation for lack of time or options.

Finally, the hundred-year-olds mentioned self-care as one of the secrets to their long life—a corollary of the last factor. They accepted the responsibility for taking care of themselves and avoided activities involving intense stress.

If science can extend our life span beyond one hundred (as it probably will one day), we should do all we can to help science along. By eliminating the frustrations, inequities, impersonality, and tensions of working for someone else, or of working for too low a wage, we can prime our bodies (and minds) to accept an extended life with grace and dignity.

The economics of freedom suggests all the elements present in the lives of those centenarians: self-employment, long hours (but confined to few days), serenity (by doing what you want to do), moderation (by balancing work with play and by not making money your primary goal), and self-care (by accepting responsibility for your own life).

If you are going to live to be one hundred—a very distinct possibility for many people alive today—I sincerely hope you live those years exactly as you wish to live them: free.

In your new life, expect change to be one of the few certainties. Right now, the industries that are on the rise and appear ripe for your efforts are energy, drugs, domestic oil, office equipment, leisure-time products, repairing, recycling, farm-equipment manufacturing and repair, inexpensive food processing, remodeling, construction, health care, broadcast media, computer software, childcare, delivery services, and social work. In time, some of these industries will peak, and new, more viable industries will emerge. Keep alert for them.

As the 1980's were the "lite" years, the 1990's will be the "green" years, with environmentally sound products and services advancing to the forefront.

The economics of freedom is a new economics, not an important part of the established order. But as you leave the old economic system, the new economics will become the established order. And freedom will ring in clearer tones and in more ears than ever.

The economics of freedom seems to be both contagious and inspirational. As one person sees another enjoying the benefits of freedom, that person becomes motivated to attempt the break from job habituation himself. And when he proves successful, his example motivates other people to opt for freedom. It's a healthy contagion, and I see it happening all around me.

I also cannot help but notice how the desire for more

freedom inspires more original thoughts about earning. As people learned I was writing this book, they began giving me their own ideas for earning money without a job.

I've been dazzled by their economic brilliance and creativity. Many of these people formerly held dull, plodding jobs and busied themselves with dull, plodding work. Yet they held in their minds the ideas for bright, interesting earning endeavors. Thank heaven, many of these folks are now doing that kind of work. And at the same time, they are enjoying more freedom, more money, and more self-fulfillment.

What prevents most people from making the transition from job earning to jobless earning? Perhaps it is lack of discipline—the discipline to go it alone, energized by one's own initiative. But I suspect it is the lack of guts to make the decision to go it alone.

No question, it is a very tough decision to make. But once you make it, things seem to fall in place, because you cause them to fall in place. If there is one common thread among the people who have succeeded without a job, it is that they agree it happened easier and faster than they imagined.

Since the original edition of this book was published (I published it myself because I wanted to control the entire process—for the fun, the experience, and the money, and I made out well on all three), I have received numerous other ideas for earning money without a job.

Many of these are included in later chapters, and my gratitude toward their contributors is offered right here. But the point is that this book cannot possibly contain *all* the neat ideas for earning money without a job.

So look around. Think original, capitalistic thoughts. You'll find and you'll dream up many more money-earning ideas. Unfortunately, many of you will also neglect to

follow up on these ideas. Many of you who wish to be free will never actually make the attempt. Why?
I'll tell you why:

1. Your family will question your decision.
2. Your friends will think you're nuts for leaving a steady job.
3. You will be frightened to try something you haven't tried before.
4. The change will come across to you as too radical.
5. You'll figure that freedom is something for other people, and jobless earning is just not something for you.
6. You're surviving without much freedom, and everything is all right.
7. It's too much trouble to make the leap from security to freedom.
8. You're not ready to make the change yet.
9. You've never tested a life filled with freedom and joyful earning.
10. It has never entered your mind that you *can* control your life.

Before you commence a life of freedom, happiness, and self-reliance, there are obstacles to overcome. I think it is crucial to deal with these obstacles, and crazy to ignore them.

Perhaps I haven't listed your particular obstacles. In that case, list them yourself. In order for you to overcome your obstacles, you've got to know them. For only if you know them can you face up to them, then conquer them.

Take heart that most people who are enjoying more money and more free time than you are had their own list of obstacles. Take heart that their list may have been a lot longer than yours. But some people want freedom so much that they are able to overcome their obstacle list. For your sake, I hope you are one of these people.

I suspect you have the makings, or else you wouldn't be reading this book in the first place. It's no coincidence that I'm writing about freedom and you're reading about freedom. It is strictly intentional on my part—*and* on yours.

To gain economic freedom, all you've got to do is know how to bring it about, and want it enough to make it happen. I'm doing my part by telling how to bring it about.

Now if you truly want it enough, it *will* happen. That combination of knowledge and desire is all it takes. Half that combination you hold in your hands. The other half you hold in your head.

Put the two together and you're on your way.

CHAPTER
TWO

Positioning Yourself

What are you all about? The answer to this should serve as your springboard to earning.

Take out a few sheets of paper and begin listing all the things about you that might possibly give you clues as to your earning potential. Begin with grammar school. Did you excel in any particular thing? Did your teachers have any especially glowing things to say about you consistently? What about your hobbies as a child?

Write everything on the list that comes to your mind. Include everything about your education, your part-time jobs, your interests, your hobbies, your skills, your past accomplishments, awards, travel, military service, notable relationships, your grades in school, contributions to the high school newspaper, athletic feats, Boy or Girl Scout accomplishments, contacts, business references, past employment, and finally—your own opinions of your strengths. Be immodest and pull out all the stops. My original list ran six single-spaced typed pages. I still have it, though I wouldn't show it to a soul.

By condensing your list into one page of your most

appropriate credentials, arranged in an orderly way, you have a fairly good representation of yourself to use in assessing your own possibilities, and to use to impress others into hiring you. From this list, you may move on to the second phase of your self-evaluation. And you'll be better prepared to answer hard questions: Do you wish to work with your brain or brawn? Do you wish to work from your home? Do you want to work alone or in combination with one or more people? Might one of these people already live in your home? How much, if any, money will you need to get started?

A good starting point for your earning is your last job. Only instead of doing it for your last company, do it for your own company if that is at all possible. Or do it for other companies on a modular basis.

Crucial point: Do you have capital or assets that may be converted to capital? If you do, you have an entire world of earning possibilities open to you, as you'll see in chapter 7. In no case will you need an immense amount of money. But $1,000 to invest in equipment can make a big difference in your earning options.

If you have no savings account, stocks, bonds, or other investments, do you have anything that you might sell to gain capital? I have sold old paintings my wife and I collected, a silver collection, an interest in a small boat, and sundry other items—just to raise money to be used to make more money. The ability to free up capital should be explored carefully.

While you're examining your money, examine your equipment on hand. You can earn money if you have tools, a car, a home, a telephone, a typewriter, adding machine, computer, word processor, VCR, video camera, darkroom, kitchen, garage, basement, stove, sewing machine, drawing board, camera, motion-picture projector, garden, or limitless other things common to an

average home. All these can be used as earning equipment, or security for a loan to purchase earning equipment. So take careful stock.

Perhaps you don't have the equipment, but you can
trade for it. The bartering principle again. And, of course,
you can buy equipment. Or rent equipment.

At this point, it's a good idea to compile your *earning
inventory.* Everyone has one. To make up yours, begin
with several sheets of blank paper. On the first sheet,
write at the top, "Things I Like to Do." That's part 1 of
your earning inventory. Fill that page with the kinds of
things that you honestly like to do. They need not be
oriented to earning money, just to things you enjoy.
Later, we'll see how they can be translated into a
healthy cash flow.

Take your time to list at least ten items here, though a
fertile imagination will enable you to list twenty things
you enjoy doing. This list is one of the most enjoyable
you'll make. Have fun making it a long one.

Part 2 of your earning inventory is called "Things I'm
Good At." This is no time to be modest. List every single
thing that has ever earned you a compliment, a dollar, a
high grade, a medal, a pat on the back. Surprisingly, most
people shortchange themselves with this list. So ask your
friends to help. Just keep in mind that the average *high
school graduate* has twenty skills by means of which he or
she can earn money. Twenty! How many will you have?
One woman I counseled could come up with about seven
things at which she considered herself competent. I asked
her to show the list to her friends. Several of them mentioned her cooking prowess, which she had neglected to
put on the list. Today, she runs a catering firm that grossed
over half a million dollars last year, but she plumb forgot
that she was a good cook. Don't take yourself for granted.

Part 3 of your earning inventory concerns the earning

tools you have right now. I've mentioned some of those just a few paragraphs back. See what you can add to the list. Again, aim for listing ten items, but do enough internal investigation so that you come up with twenty. The more tools, the wider your inventory, the broader your earning options.

Keep that earning inventory in mind when looking over the earnways listed later in this book. You'll find several earnways quite attractive once you realize you have much of the equipment for them already.

Examining your three pages of earning inventory, you can write a fourth page that has your credentials for earning money.

Take your page of credentials; draw an illustration on it that demonstrates your work (or have a friend supply the graphics in trade for a service that you might perform), and print up a small quantity. Now you have a brochure on your company.

Make up a name for that company. I call mine Jay Levinson & Partners. I explain that the company is composed of a core individual and a myriad of outside services. Such a company name does not limit me to any particular line of work. I arranged that on purpose.

It also helps, if you're a company, to have business cards, a business phone, and a listing in the Yellow Pages. Stationery is a business aid too, though I conducted my business for three years with no stationery—just plain white paper with one of those mail-order address labels affixed to the upper right corner. Finally, get a supply of invoice forms so that you can send bills out for your work.

A word about billing: It's easier than collecting. The people who are aggressive about collecting are a lot richer than those who are not aggressive. But there is no joy in collecting bills. It requires patience, persistence, and a strong sense of righteousness.

The most successful bill collector I know has collections down to a six-part process:

1. Send the original bill.
2. Two weeks later, send another bill with a cute, warm reminder that it is overdue.
3. Two weeks later, send another bill with the word OVERDUE stamped in enormous letters across the top of the bill. (This one usually gets action.)
4. Two weeks later, phone the person at his place of business.
5. Two weeks later (and this is the toughest part of all), phone the person at 3:00 A.M. at his home. This may be aggravating, but it is completely legal as long as you do not call frequently or call collect.
6. Turn the bill over to a collection agency.

My bill-collecting friend, who earns a lot more than I and hasn't had a job in twenty years, rarely has to turn any account over for collection. Still, he rates bill collecting as the ugliest part of being in his own part-time business.

Position yourself to potential customers not only as a problem solver but also as an opportunity spotter. Show how you can put out fires after they start, and how you also can expand your customer's business through methods other than mere problem solving.

Example: A friend visited tropical-fish stores and offered to clean fish tanks, which otherwise would get dirty and kill the fish, as well as turn customers away. This positioned him as a problem solver. Then he convinced the owner of one of the stores that he ought to offer fish tanks to businesses, along with fish-tank maintenance. This positioned him as an opportunity spotter. He succeeded in both endeavors. So did his customer. And so can you. It's called being aware of earning options.

In order to earn money without a job, it is necessary to organize your time, your space, and your life to accommodate all demands upon you. This means freeing up a specific number of days or hours per week that will be *primarily dedicated* to earning along the lines you wish.

Whatever you do you should be able to accomplish with excellence, or else you should not offer to do it. The economics of freedom does not allow for shabby work. In order for you to enjoy your freedom, you've got to be good enough to have earned the freedom. It may not be a job, but it's still work. And you've still got to work at it. So don't try to kid anyone, including yourself. And only engage in pursuits you can succeed in accomplishing well.

Once you are convinced that you can succeed, you'll find that nerve is an asset. All else being equal, a talented individual with guts will make out better than a talented individual without guts. The former will go after business that the latter might be hesitant about soliciting. The former will therefore get business that the latter will miss.

You've got to believe in yourself with passionate fervor. You've got to love yourself for the right reasons. And then you've got to let all that positivity come shining through.

If you've decided to pursue work that can best flourish in a big city rather than in a small town, you'd better get yourself near that big city or else decide to earn money in endeavors that do not require the options afforded by high population.

Understand that you do not need to be anywhere near a city for hundreds and hundreds of money-earning efforts. But *some* work needs the opportunities found in a city, while other work requires only the presence of a post office and little else in the way of civilization. Measure your chosen pursuits against the realities of your current geography.

Chances are, unless you can conduct your business via phone, fax, or mail, it just plain makes sense to go where the customers are. So if you live in a city and wish to be of service to farmers—or if you live in the country and wish to be of service to store owners—you'll have to relocate to earn money.

To many of us, however, relocation is a bad word. Many people live where they do because that's where they happened to be born. But that's certainly not a valid reason for staying if they're unhappy with their location.

Many other people live where they do because that's where all the jobs are. But if you have no job, you now have the freedom to pick up and live anywhere you please, as long as you can earn money there along the lines you choose. The economics of freedom permits you to select work that will enable you to live in the city or the country, near mountains or oceans, forests or desert. You can live where people ski the majority of the year. Or you can live where no snow has fallen in decades.

Align your earning desires with your living desires, and before long you will be doing just what you want to do, just where you want to be doing it. That alone is a good measure of success.

Don't limit your choices to America, either. Perhaps the United States has an overabundance of people earning money exactly as you wish to earn it. Perhaps the competition is less keen in Canada, Australia, Africa, Europe, Japan, or countless islands. Many Americans have sought and achieved their fortunes in South America . . . legally.

For three years of my life, I lived in London. During that time, my wife and I traveled like crazy, knowing that this was our big chance to see Europe. Much to our amazement, we discovered that nearly a quarter of a million Americans live in London. In fact, we discovered Americans earning a living in virtually every country we visited. Yet we both agreed wholeheartedly that the propaganda we had heard all our lives was indeed true: America is, for us, the best nation on earth from almost every standpoint.

I can think of no reason to live in any country but the United States. But for your earning endeavors, perhaps you can shop the U.N. and pick a nation better suited to your talents. Still, for your sake, I hope it is the United States.

Now here comes the single most important positioning of all. When you complete this book, make a list of all the things suggested that you might do. Make it as long a list as possible. You'll find a lot of ideas to select from, so don't be too selective at first.

Choose, say, twenty ways you may earn money without a job. From that list of twenty, narrow the list down to the ten ways you'd realistically most enjoy earning money. Then zero in on the five best ways of all. *Next, do all five.*

In other words, don't keep narrowing the list any more. Don't leave yourself with one source of income. Five is a much better number. It can quintuple your income, your security, and your long-term possibilities. Perhaps later, one way will become clearly apparent as a prime area for your energies. But until that time, go in five different directions at once. As I write this, I earn money from nine different sources. Again, that happened because I made it happen. Of the nine, some require a few minutes a month to maintain; others require a few hours a week. But I've got nine things going for me. And they all help. Believe me, when you have no job, this isn't greed; it's survival in a tough economy. And it works.

If you stay with your list of ten earning possibilities, and follow all ten, even if you only earn $200 per possibility per month, that's a hefty $2,000-per-month income, and if you play it right, you only have to work a few days a week.

By not expecting a large income from one, you can aim to earn a small income from many. And that does wonders for the insecurity that goes along with freedom.

Again, the hardest part is setting up these income sources. But once they are set up, they can become automatic. And you can easily stand the loss of any one.

Understand that you *will* lose sources of income. Failure is a big part of earning money without a job, but not as large a part as success. If you establish five sources of income, you can realistically figure that three of those sources will not work out in the course of a year, leaving you with two sources of income.

Activate a second five sources. Again, three will fall flat while two will take wing and soar. Now you've got four sources of income. Want more? Launch another five enterprises. Steel yourself against the virtually inevitable failure of three of them. No problem. Two more will bring in the bucks. Now you've got *six sources of income.*

Is six enough? For many people, yes. But I need nine. I don't need them for the sake of greed. Just chalk it up to gracious survival. Sometimes I've had as many as fourteen sources of income. Other times, I've made do with four.

At one point in my life, I had two rather large sources of income. I hardly worked at all, after the initial stages. And I was earning $4,000 per month from just these two sources. Loads of freedom. Loads of money. And then that monster Murphy laid down his law and I was suddenly down to no sources of income and no money. No fault of my own, either.

So I said, "no more"—and I learned much of what I state in this book, especially in this chapter. Earn your keep via several sources so that you are never dependent upon one or two sources. For if you are dependent, you are not free.

If your list of potential sources numbers fifty, and you earn a measly $100 per source, you are bringing in $5,000 per month. For someone with no job, that's not terrible.

Of course, it's unrealistic to expect all fifty sources to come through, but it is the lofty target you set your sights on. As the late Leo Burnett, one of America's most outstanding advertising men, stated as a company motto: "If you reach for the stars, you might not get one, but you're not likely to come up with a handful of mud, either."

Once you are satisfied that you have positioned yourself properly—that is to say honestly, realistically, and opportunistically—you must decide whether you are going to operate as a proprietor, a partnership, or a corporation.

This is an important decision and bears much consideration, both on your part and on the part of your attorney. I have always been a proprietorship, because I try to protect myself from red tape as much as possible. This has been very satisfying. But this is not to say it has been wise.

As a proprietorship, I was able to get organized almost instantly. I was able to avoid legal expenses, and time-consuming waits for bureaucratic action and paperwork. Those were the good things. Here were the risks: (1) I was personally and completely responsible for debts, obligations, and liabilities incurred. Knowing this, I was extremely careful, and still am, about incurring debts, obligations, and liabilities. The fact that I am a proprietorship may have forced me to become more conservative than I am normally. (2) My business income was income directly to me, which offered me less shelter from the tax man than other methods of setting up my business. Still,

I have no regrets, and I have been intentionally careful about avoiding one of the many pitfalls that await sole proprietors. I have also avoided income-earning endeavors that might incur liability to myself.

Had I set up a partnership (and this might seem normal for a company called Jay Levinson & Partners), I would have run the identical risks of being a proprietor, *plus* I would have run the risk of my partners' incurring debts, obligations, and liabilities. In a partnership, each partner is responsible for the entire business. If a judgment were rendered against the business, and one partner couldn't pay his share, the other partner (or partners) would be liable for it. There is also a humongous number of other personal-type problems that come up in a partnership.

Some partnerships are composed of active partners only—people who are directly involved in the business. Other partnerships have a combination of active partners and inactive or limited partners. These cases are usually those where someone does the work and someone else comes up with the money. My recommendation, unless you have an active partner who is good at all those things at which you are not good, is to steer clear of a partnership.

That means that you should give careful thought to forming a corporation. Right off, you should realize that forming one will cost you money, will wrap you up in red tape, and will bog you down with bureaucratic details. Nonetheless, it may be worth the time, tape, and legal expense.

Gerardo Joffe, author of *How You Too Can Make at Least $1 Million (But Probably Much More) in the Mail-Order Business*, says, "You may have seen books advertised that promise to show you how to form your own corporation for $50. My advice: don't! If you are a do-it-yourself addict, take out your own gall bladder or something, but if you are serious about going into business, let an attorney help you with the formalities required."

I do not argue this point with Mr. Joffe, who not only has made his first million practicing the economics of freedom, but also is already well on the way toward his tenth million, every penny well deserved.

When you form a corporation, you will not be personally liable for any debts or obligations of the corporation, except in very special circumstances. Your profits will be taxed at the corporate (and more favorable) rate, and you will be able to regulate your own salary so as to optimize both your tax situation and your net income. You can help yourself even more if you form a Subchapter S corporation at the outset of your business. A Subchapter S corporation especially helps you in the beginning of your business. Get more details on this from your lawyer.

Your lawyer can also explain that a corporation helps you with federal income taxes, pension plans, deferred compensation plans, and more. She'll tell you also that as a corporation, you will be required to hold directors' and stockholders' meetings, keep minutes of the meetings, and put up with a few other formalities. She may even recommend that you incorporate in a place other than your location—say, Delaware or the Cayman Islands. Ideally, her advice will be brilliant and pertinent. And ideally, you will learn about dividends, trust funds, naming your company, and other juicy (and necessary) tidbits crucial to survival with maximum money and maximum freedom—for yourself and for your children, if any.

The selection of your lawyer is as important as the selection of your accountant. Both will be almost crucial to your success, especially in the beginning. Your accountant can save you a fortune in federal, state, and local taxes. Like your lawyer, he should be selected because he is lean, hungry, intelligent, delighted to get your business, and possessed of a chemistry that is totally compatible with your own. Select carefully. A lot depends upon it.

Your accountant can tell you how to save large amounts of money as a practitioner of the economics of freedom through legitimate expenses and deductions. He can help you obtain loans (more about this in a moment) and, perhaps of greatest importance, he can help you set up a professional system of record keeping. There is a direct correlation between accurate records and high profits. Sometimes it is only the lack of accurate records that separates an entrepreneur from success. Don't let this minor (not really minor if you do it wrong) chore prevent you from achieving your goals.

Along with your lawyer and your accountant, develop a warm relationship with a banker. The banker with whom you should start relating is your current personal banker. It is her business to lend money to people and businesses and turn a profit for her bank. The key phrase there is "to lend money." That is her job and, believe me, she wants to say yes far more than she wants to say no.

So give her every reason in the world to say yes to you when you come to her for money. How to get her to be agreeable? Present her with a business plan, a financial statement (called a balance sheet), and a projected statement (called a *pro forma*). Also present her with a descriptive letter of what your company is and does, what your product or service is and does, and a statement about yourself.

Be honest with your banker; relate to her as a human being; and remember that she *wants* to lend you money so that *she* can make money from your skill and talent.

If your current banker seems cold, unreasonable, or unintelligent, shop around for another. Check for the following: understanding of the small businessperson, range of services, check-depositing charges, minimum balances expected, and sense of humanity. I believe that there are few differences in banks, but many differences in bankers. One of the low moments of my banking relationship occurred when my favorite banker was promoted to a distant branch. Once my Charlie was gone, the bank just never seemed the same. And as a result, I had to switch banks.

Beyond banks and loan companies (beware of loan companies) there are many lending institutions. Perhaps the most obvious, yet frequently overlooked, is the government. A Small Business Administration loan is a lot easier to get than one might imagine. But don't necessarily turn there first. Ask your accountant.

Don't hold high expectations for venture capitalists. Although they are the glamour lenders, they say "no" to more than 99 percent of the people who ask them for money. In the U.S. the vast majority of people obtain money either from banks or from friends and/or relatives. If these sources don't pan out, people give up.

Don't you give up. Instead, seek alternative sources of financing. Consider leasing, getting a home equity loan, or good old (but tough) bootstrap financing—saving the money you require from your earnings. Not easy, but quite common. You move more slowly, but incur fewer debts.

You may have heard that one of the biggest reasons for companies' failing is undercapitalization. This is not true, however. Mismanagement, failure to market aggressively, and an inability to deal with growth cause more business failures than undercapitalization.

Kurt Vonnegut, Jr., writes of the money river. The money river is a flow of information that is available to only a minuscule number of people. The information in the flow is such that it can result in an amazing return on your investment. But very few have access to the flow. I hope that your accountant will in some way connect up with the money river, and that you will, in due time, become a tributary. Until that time, your money manager should at least be able to grant you access to the money rivulet.

Okay. Now you've done the things your lawyer, accountant, and banker have asked. You are nearly all positioned. Just a few more things to get in order.

Who is going to answer your phone when you're out? You can ask someone in your household to do it. You can get an answering device, you can use voice mail, or you can get an answering service. You can even ignore the question and just take calls when you are at home.

By now, I must consider myself an expert on the topic, since I have experimented with all the above phone answerers. My wife hated only one of the options—the one where someone in the household answers. She claimed to be spending more time taking messages than doing anything else. The other options seemed equally desirable. But right now, I use a simple answering machine—accurate, friendly, and relatively inexpensive. And people no longer resent such electronic communication.

On mail, take the time to talk to your local postmaster. You'll find him or her to be extremely helpful in the matters of saving postage and shipping costs and packaging hassles.

If you are setting up an office in your home, be sure you have enough storage space for whatever you need to store. If you don't, make arrangements. And if you do work from your home, set up your office as professionally as if you were setting it up in an office building. That is, make it efficient in its arrangement and flexible to fit your needs now and in the future. There are books that map out ideal home offices. You'll find some listed at the end of this book.

Don't forget to check out your chamber of commerce and tell someone there of your plans. From the chamber, you can learn peculiarities of your own town or county, special advantages, local disadvantages, the competitive situation, potential customers, and laws of which you must be aware. Do you need a business license? A fictitious-name statement? Do you need private postal carriers? Cut Murphy off at the pass, and obtain this information out front—as much information as possible.

One final word about positioning: I have positioned myself in a large home on a hillside overlooking San Francisco Bay. My positioning includes a warmly heated swimming pool, a live-in housekeeper, a wife with a taste for classy clothes, and a daughter who gives birth to grandchildren deserving of all the toys in the store. Such positioning forces motivation upon me. And as a result, I scramble that much harder. With a one-bedroom apartment in Milwaukee, there would be a lot less motivation and a lot less scrambling.

But I've positioned myself as I do on purpose. It's sort of like hanging a carrot on a stick in front of a donkey. Only I'm enjoying the carrot as I strive for it.

Strain, yes. Regrets, no.

CHAPTER THREE

Obtaining Business

Once you decide what you can do, will do, and want to do, you're all set for the final phase—doing it.

Your prime requirements now are energy, persistence, patience, positivity, a thick skin, and flexibility. You also need some sense of realism.

The best place to begin scouting out customers is among your contacts. Contacts are friends, acquaintances, business associates, ex-schoolmates, ex-associates, friends of friends, friends of associates, businesses you patronize, neighbors, strangers you meet at a party, fishing buddies, fellow members of teams (bowling, softball, bridge, whatever), fellow club members, and anyone else who isn't a total stranger.

You can vastly enlarge your circle of contacts by joining organizations: social, athletic, golf, professional, community, anything. Many businesses have been built strictly as a result of contacts made by the intentional joining of an organization to make contacts.

I purposely have been a nonjoiner. I well realize the value of contacts and the wide availability of potential customers in clubs that I might have joined. But I dislike crowds; I feel slightly shabby joining an organization with the main purpose of making business contacts; and I don't get on well with the formality that's concomitant with most organizations. This joining avoidance has hurt me in the pocketbook. But I'm willing to sacrifice the income for the freedom from artificial contacts. My problem.

Another excellent way to develop contacts is by personal appearances at the office of your potential contact. By engaging in face-to-face contact, you become a lot closer than a telephone or correspondence contact enables you to become. During your personal contact, you should naturally try to impress a customer with your credentials, abilities, talents, and energy. But more important—get him to *like* you.

If you impress a person as being someone who is good to have around, good to do business with, pleasant to deal with—you're just about home free. Unfortunately, being liked is more important than being proficient. That's why personal contacts help so much. That's why personal calls have such successful results. So show how you can handle the work with excellence. But do it in as lovable a way as possible.

The economics of freedom permits you to do a bit of your own horn blowing, as well. As an employee with a job, there is really little need, if any, for you to talk up your work. In fact, it might be just the wrong thing to do. As a free soul with no job but with the ability to earn money along several lines, there is a need and reason for you to speak freely of your work.

Whenever possible, tell people what you do and, if you can keep within bounds of good taste, how well you do it. This can be accomplished by relating before-and-after stories, by detailing your experience in your field, by rattling off references to your ability, and by showing what you do.

It's all word-of-mouth advertising, even if the words happen to come from your mouth.

There is nothing sinful about selling yourself, and the economics of freedom dictates that self-praise is a near virtue.

Besides personal contacts, personal calls, and personal testimonials, how else can you spread the word about your capabilities? Well, there are phone calls. A persistent and conscientious practitioner of the economics of freedom can make a dozen phone calls per hour, easily. And that permits a five-minute conversation, long enough to get in all the facts and goodies about yourself, your service, or your product.

Getting it all in during your initial contact is a good idea. It may be your *only* contact, so it's no time to be subtle or modest. And although a phone call is less personal than a visit, it is easier, less expensive, more conducive to mass efforts, and still it is personal to a degree. Working an eight-hour day at twelve phone calls per hour gives you ninety-six contacts per day. And even with a three-day week, that's an enormous number of contacts and an almost certain possibility of success.

With just a bare minimum of luck, three days of phoning can result in one month's worth of work.

If you're good on the phone, all the better. If you're not, it's intelligent to prepare a script to use as a guide. Memorize the words of the script as well as the ideas, but be sure none of it sounds memorized.

A well-planned phone presentation requires that you present everything you have to say in an organized fashion, that you listen to and hear what the party on the other end is saying, and that you wrap up the conversation in a clear conclusion. It is hoped that this conclusion will detail the next step—either a personal visit, or a fulfillment of the work itself.

I am an absolute loser on the phone. I can plan my presentation, deliver it flawlessly, and still I don't get the results that I do with letters. Perhaps that's because I write better than I speak.

I have a friend who makes 100 percent of his contacts by phone, works part-time, and easily clears $3,000 per month via this method. When he tried writing letters, he struck out. Perhaps he speaks better than he writes.

Probably you'll find that a combination of visiting, phoning, and writing will strike the best balance, but you still should tilt your efforts in the direction of your talents and in the direction that feels best to you.

Writing individual letters is another way to herald yourself. The letters should be written regularly and creatively. You can't hope to write and mail as many letters as you can make phone calls (unless you embark upon a mass direct-mail effort). But a personal letter, one of a kind, can open doors that a phone conversation won't open.

While we're on the subject of mail, direct mail is a medium to consider. If it is simple to obtain a list of your potential clients—either from the Yellow Pages, a business directory, or by buying the list from a direct-mail-list broker (see "mailing lists" in the Yellow Pages)—you should consider using direct mail. But keep in mind that most people refer to it as junk mail. And they've probably got a good reason for doing so.

So don't make yours junky. A friend of mine recently conducted a mailing with great success. Upon the envelope she had printed in large, black letters: "This is not junk mail." Right to the point.

When you boiled your credentials down to one page, you created a brochure/circular/advertisement on yourself. Naturally, you should enclose one with each personal letter you write. You should include one with any direct-mail effort. And of course you should leave one with each customer to whom you pay a personal visit.

But do more, as well. Distribute your circulars in places where customers are likely to be found. It may be on downtown street corners. Perhaps it is in office buildings, theater lobbies, lines to get into the movies or onto the bus. It might behoove you to place your circular under windshield wipers of cars parked in a particular place— such as the parking lot of a shopping center, a baseball diamond, a do-it-yourself store or in a commuters' parking area. Use your imagination.

You can distribute your brochures in mailboxes, under doorsteps, or at stoplights where cars tend to congregate. Be certain that it is legal to distribute where you intend to distribute. And know that by disseminating information about yourself by this method, you are saving a lot of money by not advertising.

The following circular, found in our mailbox, netted the writer our business:

Joel Does It All!

Need gardening or tree-trimming? Joel does it!
Need electrical work or masonry? Joel does it!
Need roofing or any carpentry? Joel does it!
Need hauling or major cleaning? Joel does it!
Need window-washing or painting? Joel does it!

Since 1970, Joel has been serving the needs of home-owners in this community, whatever those needs may be. Joel is reliable, honest, professional, friendly, and extremely efficient.

Best of all, Joel's prices are far less than you'd expect. For a free estimate on gardening, tree trimming, electrical work, masonry, roofing, carpentry, hauling, major cleaning, window washing, painting, or almost any task, call Joel at 383-1073.

**Joel-of-All-Trades
383-1073**

It costs just pennies per circular, even a fraction of a penny if you do your homework and find a reasonable printer. And don't forget to include your address and phone number. People may not respond to your circular at first, but many will save it to refer to a few months in the future. It works the same way with advertising: not a lot of immediate response, but a healthy residual effect.

Advertising is, of course, the most common method of obtaining business. It is the most expensive or least expensive, depending upon the kind of advertisement you create. A good ad, designed to make your product or service interesting, designed to attract attention, designed to motivate people to become your customers—that's inexpensive advertising.

On the other hand, any advertising that does not attract customers is expensive advertising, regardless of its cost.

I spent four years of my life teaching advertising on the college level. It is therefore difficult for me to tell you all you need to know about it as one tiny part of one chapter in one book. Still, allow me to try.

The single most motivating factor in attracting people to a service, store, or product is *confidence*. Good advertising breeds confidence. Regular advertising breeds confidence. A well-planned ad or commercial, run frequently, has the effect of making your offering a *good friend*. And people buy from good friends. So if you have a limited budget to spend on advertising, unless there is a pressing reason to spend it with one big splash—spend it on regularly appearing ads or regularly running commercials. Don't expect a crashing instant response. But expect some instant response. Expect some long-lasting response. Expect people to begin to know who you are and what you are offering. Expect people to have heard of you when you call upon them by phone, personal visit, or correspondence. Expect people to develop confidence in you.

Whether you create your own ad or use a professional person or company to help you with it, be sure you are clearly communicating something. Plan your ad or commercial (TV commercials are now amazingly inexpensive to run) around an *idea*. Decide what you want to communicate before you begin creating the ad. And don't get carried away with cleverness.

Instead, communicate the most inherently interesting thing about your product, service, or store. Communicate the most important benefit of becoming a customer of yours. Be sure your ad is believable, and be sure it has *something* about it to make it stand out from all the other ads in the medium you select.

For keeping expenses down, the best media are local newspapers and local radio stations. And often these are the only media you should employ. But look into local TV as well, especially cable TV. In San Francisco, a cable-TV outfit offers sixty seconds of commercial time to a potential audience of forty thousand for $6. And that's the whole cost. So don't think that all TV costs a fortune. Remember, too, that TV is the best medium anywhere for *demonstrating* a product, service, or feature—and that TV ordinarily reaches the most people. Also keep in mind that most advertising agencies charge you nothing for their services, and are compensated by receiving a 15 percent discount from the media they employ. So if you decide to advertise in order to obtain business, talk to a professional. It can save you a lot of money.

Consider using the classified section to advertise. It has the advantage of talking to people who are looking for something to buy in the first place—just like the Yellow Pages. And realize that if you advertise in the Yellow Pages, you can appear every bit as large and successful as your biggest competitor—something you cannot do in other media.

While on the topic of advertising, I want to call your attention to the vast amount of terrible advertising in most media. That terrible advertising is an advantage to you if you create advertising that is better than terrible. Remember, as a guide to anything you advertise: Women do not buy shampoo; instead, women buy beautiful hair.

A concept to remember for obtaining business is to save money for your customers by doing exactly what other, larger, companies do, but doing it for less money. Your lack of overhead will enable you to gain this competitive edge, and the clear appeal you can make (saving money) will obtain some business for you in short order. Then, if you do your job well, word-of-mouth advertising will establish confidence in your offering, and you may be off and running. Just be careful you don't become a big company and require a big overhead yourself.

You will have the option to become a big company if you simply comprehend the incredible power of marketing. Up to this point, we've been talking about advertising, which is only a tiny fraction of marketing.

Marketing puts at least one hundred weapons at your disposal. Advertising is one of them. Direct mail is one of them. So is canvassing, making personal phone calls, and joining clubs. But there are many others worthy of your examination. To continue in my own quest to earn money without a job, I urge you to read my marketing books, *Guerrilla Marketing, Guerrilla Marketing Attack,* and

Guerrilla Marketing Weapons, to get the details and the full list of weapons available to the entrepreneur.

Of the one hundred weapons of marketing, use as many as you can use properly. Half of them are *completely free.* Guerrilla marketing dictates that you invest time, energy, and imagination in the marketing process, not merely money.

It also demands that you memorize, then live by, eight words that should govern your marketing. Just to help you remember them, all eight of the words end in the letters "ent."

1. The first word is "commitment." And that's what really makes marketing work. Develop a simple marketing plan. Then commit to it. A fair marketing plan with commitment will produce far more profits than a brilliant plan without commitment.

2. The second word is "investment," for that's what marketing really is—a conservative investment that's better than anything offered by a bank or investment house, but still an investment, not a miracle worker. Keep that in mind and you'll never walk away from your investment.

3. The third word is "consistent," because if you keep changing your ads and marketing and media around, your prospects won't be able to understand what you're all about. Give them the sense that you know what you're doing. Consistent marketing will do that for you. Of course, you also have to really know what you're doing.

4. The fourth word you already know. It's "confident"—confidence is the single factor that influences sales above all others. Even above quality, service, and price? Right, above all, consumers patronize businesses in which

they are confident. It's interesting to sit back a moment and realize that your commitment will make them confident; your treatment of marketing as investment will make them confident; and your being consistent with regard to your identity, your media, and your positioning will make them confident.

5. The fifth word is something you must be to practice this commitment. It is "patient"—patience is the single most important attribute of the person who runs successful marketing programs. I've worked with *Fortune* 500 firms and teensy start-ups. The profitable ones have patient captains at the helm.

6. The sixth word is "convenient," because these days, more than ever before, people want to do business with firms that will make everything easy. These firms have extended hours, extended days, easy payment plans, delivery, and a powerful orientation to service. They also accept every credit card under the sun. They knock themselves out being convenient. If you don't you're going to have a tough time in the nineties and beyond.

7. The seventh word is "assortment." Marketing isn't advertising or location or sales representatives. It's a gigantic assortment of one hundred weapons—all winning the battle for the customer. The wider your assortment of weapons, the broader your grin when you review your bank balance. Don't say I didn't alert you to this new fact of life in the world of marketing.

8. The eighth word is "subsequent," meaning that marketing doesn't end when you've made a sale. The marketing you do subsequent to the sale is the marketing that pays the richest dividends. That's when the winners do their best and their heaviest marketing. They know, and now you know, that it costs one-fifth as much to sell to a current customer as to sell to a new one. They know that customers have this endearing way of becom-

ing repeat customers and sending in a parade of referral customers.

Commitment. Investment. Consistent. Confident. Patient. Convenient. Assortment. Subsequent. Don't forget these eight words if you wish to succeed at jobless earning. Freedom comes only to those who are willing to work to win it. And breathing life into those eight words and concepts will mean freedom to you. I promise. And I warn you that *seven* out of eight won't cut the mustard. Got that?

Regardless of how many sources of income you develop, each will require marketing. And for each you will have three markets: your *universe*—people who have any possibility of buying what you will be selling; your *prospects*—folks who are quite likely to buy what you sell; and your *customers*—those beloved creatures who have already discovered you. The rule of thumb says you should invest 10 percent of your marketing budget talking to your universe, 30 percent talking to your prospects, and 60 percent talking to your customers.

This means that your sacred obligation is to constantly move members of the universe to your prospect list, and prospects to your customer list, and that you should be selling with high energy to your customers. From such rules of thumb come small—and large—fortunes.

Once you have established some possible income sources, take a walk, ride a bike, or drive a car down commercial streets (or residential streets if residential occupants are your audience) just looking for problems, opportunities, potential customers, possible modular relationships and needs that are begging to be filled. Cruising the streets with this awareness foremost in your consciousness can lead to surprising and profitable results.

Possibly the most fruitful source of new business opportunities for you will again be the Yellow Pages. Study them as though you were reading a best-seller, and keep an eagle eye peeled for potential associations. Together with the daily paper, the Yellow Pages can suggest endless ideas and provide you with lists of possible customers. The leads you can get are countless.

Innumerable leads and valuable information may be obtained directly from the federal government. Departments of the government—agriculture, interior, commerce, and many other agencies—are loaded with informative pamphlets describing work that needs to be done, methods of succeeding at many endeavors, and lines of work that you may never have even considered. In your area, check the United States Federal Information Center, the Federal Job Information Center, and the Government Printing Office to enter the bureaucracy-laden, but delightfully informative, world of government-offered information.

After you have examined the resources of the federal government, look into your own state, county, and city government to see if they can shed more light on methods by which you may earn money without a job. Their data is also rich with good earning ideas.

Your own local chamber of commerce, as previously mentioned, can be of further help, as can the classified pages of your Sunday paper, local advertising, postings in public places, and business-opportunity magazines such as *Entrepreneur*.

But always look to yourself as the main starting point. Look to the things that you enjoy doing and the things at which you are excellent. Remember that those are the basic tools for success in the economics of freedom. Relate these likes and skills to the needs of the marketplace as best you can, and your success will be as emotionally satisfying as it is financially rewarding.

Once you have decided on the business or businesses that will support you in the style to which you'd like to become accustomed, recognize what it takes for you to succeed with your customers. That part is easy. If your customer is an individual, to succeed you need only be superb at what you are offering. But if your customer is a business, you should relate your story to *increasing the businessperson's profitability.* You can obtain business from virtually anyone *if* you can increase profits. You can talk about service and sales and traffic and competitiveness to him all you like. But your prime benefit will be that you can increase his bottom-line profits. And if you can, there is hardly any way that he can say no to your offering. So be sure your offering *can* help his profitability. Then prove it. You can accomplish this if you can be solution-oriented to businesses with problems—or opportunity-oriented to businesses with no apparent problems.

And remember, businesses aren't the only entities with problems. *People* have problems, too. And if you can solve their problems, you may just have a steady source of income. Problems that constantly need solving are: alcoholism, smoking, obesity, loneliness, sexual hang-ups, insomnia, back pain, parenting, marital troubles, insufficient income, inability to land a job, and inability to get promoted.

If you can position yourself to solve any of those problems through products, counseling, seminars, newsletters, classes, self-help efforts, clubs of people with similar problems, or any other means, you can obtain an automatic source of business just because many people are desperately searching for solutions.

Understand that you do not have to have the expertise to provide the solutions. You only have to direct the people with the problems to the people with the solutions.

And as the middleman or -woman (*solution catalyst* is a better expression), you can and should profit.

Business can also be obtained directly from your library. If that sounds like an oversimplification, I can assure you that it is not.

If you spend enough time at your library studying an income-producing venture such as poker playing, you can earn money without a job, and if you have the nerves for it, you can have a whale of a time earning. *The Education of a Poker Player* by Herbert O. Yardley is a good book with which to begin. But from there, you've got to graduate to several other books, and you've got to understand every idea, every theory they espouse. Poker is not an easy way to earn a living. But a lot of people earn their *only* money by playing the game. And you can be sure they're good.

Blackjack is another legal method of earning a living, especially in Las Vegas. An entrepreneur buddy of mine is actually barred from playing in many Nevada casinos. Where he is recognized on sight, he is unwelcome. Not because he cheats, but because he's good.

This man studied the intricacies of blackjack, all of which are painstakingly presented in library tomes. If you can memorize the rules they set down, and follow them to the letter, you can hardly lose at blackjack. But if the dealer sees that you are a true blackjack expert, one who actually can play so that the odds favor you, don't be surprised if you are invited to leave.

I wish the same expertise could be used to win at the races, but friends of mine who have earned a living at blackjack and poker report that they have been unable to earn the same living playing the horses. Too many outside variables, they report. Sad, if you love the track.

The library is a source of information on more than just poker and blackjack. It can tell you how to earn money via many methods, how to create many products (the inventor of the best-selling copper cleaner in the United States got the formula from a library book), and how to become proficient in many lines of work. Get a library card if you don't yet have one, and spend at least one day browsing. What you will learn in that one day about obtaining business will amaze you.

At the library you can also learn how to earn money just by going to college—if you're a veteran. A phone call to your nearest Veterans Administration Office can give you that information as well.

These days, more and more consciousness-raising programs are being offered as part of college curricula. Some of these programs show you how to take control of your own life, a concept heartily endorsed in the economics of freedom. Others deal with achieving financial success through increased self-insight.

It is a good idea to check with your local colleges to see if and when some of these seminars will be available in your community. If you can attend, it might be enlightening—if only to show you how amazingly possible financial freedom really is, and how much this freedom is within your province to select.

The Entrepreneurs Institute, 2392 Morse Avenue, Irvine, California 92713, is one of several businesses that offer books, cassettes, and traveling seminars on virtually all aspects of setting up your own business.

You might check when one of their seminars is going to be held in your area next, or you may try to dig up some of the several other companies that also offer mobile training programs. Many colleges offer such seminars in the evening. Look around.

Be sure you align your expectations with your local needs. Jacuzzi hot tubs have become a big business in my area. Noting this, an enterprising individual established a hot-tub servicing company: instant success. Naturally, this business would not fare so well where hot tubs are unknown. But in every area, new trends in purchasing call for the establishment of new service businesses. Your local newspaper, especially the Sunday paper, keeps you abreast of local trends and helps you become attuned to local needs. The more sensitively you are attuned, the more rapidly you will succeed. Is it really that simple? Nearly.

If a new housing tract is being built, you can be the first to offer the houseowners all the services they'll need. If a new industrial park is under construction, it is a signal for you to create a business to fill the needs of the future employee population. In the economics of freedom, the growth of other businesses provides more options for you to grow. So keep a sharp eye on growth within your community.

And don't feel bad if you miss out. If you aren't the first to offer the product or service you'll provide, you can be the first in the next housing tract, industrial park, or commercial street.

If you truly desire to become your own employer in a business of your own choosing, it is very difficult to miss out on your aims. People do not fail—they only quit trying.

Whether you decide to obtain business via advertising, making contacts, writing letters, telephoning, cruising commercial streets, paying personal calls, or any other marketing method, you will need persistence.

In the economics of freedom, persistence will be one of your most precious attributes. According to the leading salesmen in the country, it takes 4.3 attempts to close a sale before you actually succeed. The first attempt at obtaining business removes you from the ranks of strangers. The second attempt lifts you into the realm of acquaintance. The third might enable you to now list your prospect as a contact. The fourth may actually be your first attempt to make a sale to a contact. The fifth can be the one when the sale takes place, if it does take place at all. And that's just average. So you can see the crucial need for persistence.

To prove my point, I would like to quote not from a great writer, director, educator, businessman, or statesman. Instead, I quote from an ad run by McDonald's, the hamburger people:

Press On.
Nothing in the World Can
Take the Place of Persistence.
Talent Will Not; Nothing Is
More Common Than Unsuccessful
Men with Talent.
Genius Will Not; Unrewarded
Genius Is Almost a Proverb.
Education Alone Will Not;
the World Is Full of
Educated Derelicts. Persistence
and Determination Alone
Are Omnipotent.

With "Over [however many] billion sold," I cannot knock the philosophy of McDonald's. We should all sell so many of whatever we're selling.

I get a small rush of excitement every time I check my

mailbox. There is always the possibility that it contains good news. I arranged it that way on purpose, and I love it that way. Along with bills, direct-mail pieces, trade publications, consumer magazines, and personal mail, my mailbox might contain a letter or a check from a client I wrote to months back. It might contain an offer to do something I have been trying to do by phone or mail. It might contain an acceptance of a proposition, an invitation to work, a counterproposition. My mailbox is a constant source of the potential for good news and I'm almost at the point where I can live by the good news (and checks) in my mailbox. This is a delightful position to be in, and let me tell you—it took a load of letters and phone calls and persistence to make my mailbox synonymous with joy.

I strongly suggest that you do the same. You can, by establishing several potential sources of income, and then trying every single method outlined in this chapter to obtain business. In fact, if you have enough potential income sources, and you try enough ways to obtain business, it is difficult to see how you can miss earning good money while maintaining your freedom at the same time.

Set your sights high when establishing your goals. Although the idea of earning money without a job sounds a bit scary, as it should, you will find that with enough planning and determination, you will gain just what you seek.

Be prepared to live with slowness initially, but do aim high: in your amount of freedom, your income, and your growth plans.

You also will find that success comes easier if you specialize in something. This specialization will free you from much competition, and will create more awareness of your offering. More, it will make you unique, and uniqueness seems to connect up comfortably with success.

To make it as your own person, you desperately need

a sense of reality. This does not mean a sense of doom, but it does mean that dreams alone won't do the job. It means being as objective as possible, yet optimistic at the same time. It means not deluding yourself. A sense of reality will be your greatest ally when embarking upon your journey to freedom.

A final note regarding obtaining business. The more you align your income sources with the nitty-gritty of life, the more likely you are to obtain business. Stay with the fundamentals; stay away from the unnecessaries; stay with the big numbers; stay away from the small potential audiences; stay close to the earth and away from the untried, and you will be putting the probabilities on your side.

On a radio interview show, a militant radical was asked about the chances of an impending economic downfall. He answered that a downfall was sure to come and that the food business was the best business in which to be. When asked why, he stated that the food business would stay around twenty-four hours longer than any other business. While his timing may have been exaggerated, he cannot be faulted for being out of touch with the nitty-gritty.

Whatever you set yourself up to be, keep the basic needs of humanity in mind and you'll find it a lot easier to obtain business in any economic climate.

CHAPTER FOUR

Knowledge You'll Need

I have a good friend who has the uncanny ability to earn lots and lots of money. He earns it without a job. But the most amazing thing about him is the incredible accuracy and wisdom of his business advice.

He gives the best and the least business advice of any successful person I know. And these days, with so much bad business advice floating around, it is a pleasure to have a source of good advice.

My friend seems able to understand rapidly and clearly the reality of most business situations. And he's able to translate that reality into real money. Figures and all. Few people I have met possessed so keen a facility.

By understanding all, not some, of the business implications of any earning endeavor, my friend can transcend the emotion, the ego, the inefficiency, the games, and the unnecessary traditions that hamper much of business. How he does this is quite awesome to me. That he does it is quite revealing. If it can be done, it can be learned. Yet it is called good business instinct.

If you can develop instinct, you can protect yourself

from wasted time and money. Equally interesting, you can make yourself susceptible to earning money. Lots and lots of money.

Without this business instinct, you can devote your energies to a vast multitude of earning endeavors yet earn little more than gas pains. With this business instinct, plus several sources of income, you ought to be able to earn considerably more money than you really need.

With this business instinct, plus several sources of income, *plus* the intelligence to think up new sources of income and the energy to cause them to happen, you can hardly help but earn lots and lots of money. But be careful you don't expend so much energy you end up damaging your essential "you-ness."

The development of a keen business instinct and the creation of several sources of income certainly constitute the basics of earning in the economics of freedom. By comparison, other earning principles take on the stature of mere hints. Still, every principle or hint you put into practice can make a tangible difference in your income. Some even do wonders to eliminate gas pains.

The main knowledge you'll need is knowing the difference between reality and games.

If you've been working in any corporate structure, you've been protected from reality for the sake of efficiency. This is wise corporate policy.

Now start looking around and develop a sensitivity to time spent with corporate purpose foremost in mind, in contrast to time spent playing unnecessary games. Decisions are hard to come by, and much make-work fills in the gaps between necessities. The inertia places us in a dazed state where we are fully aware only a few minutes per hour. The rest of the time we're only semiaware.

While our brains cannot handle sixty minutes per hour of full-scale activity, we can increase our awareness. Just knowing *that* might do the trick if you try.

You'll need this knowledge, plus the things behind the doors it opens, in a life without a job. It will help you avoid games and spend all your earning energy in a true earning reality.

In addition to this esoteric knowledge, you'll need the hard-core knowledge of at least one trade. More than one is desirable. It does take time. It does take conscientiousness. It does take mental energy. But you're going to be around a long time, so don't impose any artificial limitations upon your essence.

Because earning money without a job is so immensely sweeping an opportunity, reading about it can only begin to bring idea patterns into your head.

What ideas do these trades stimulate in your own mind? Glazing. Masonry. Locksmithing. Blacksmithing. Plumbing. Soil conditioning. Ironing. Flooring. Sewing. Painting. Hauling. Pruning. Erosion control. Retaining-wall construction. Barbecue-pit construction. Cooking. Candle making. Piano moving. Roofing. Sandblasting. Antique restoration. Concrete work. Electrical work. Carpentry. Real estate. Underwater work. Survival instruction. First-aid instruction. Paramedical work. Paralegal work. Fireplace consultant, insulation consultant, solar energy consultant. Contractor. Engineer. Lens aluminizer. Technician. Publicist. Financial-control analyst. And a whole lot more. I know people who earn money *without* a job doing all of these things—and many others.

There is work, not just jobs, in all these trades. More in some than others. But then again, you will be interested in some of these endeavors more than others.

Wherever you end up, don't stop there. Take the time

and go through the steps of learning and becoming good at what you do, but keep yourself open-minded and forward-looking.

Buy, read, study, cherish, and understand all the implications of any version of the *Whole Earth Catalog*. In it, you will learn more about the realities of freedom than I can tell you here. And of paramount importance, learn how to cope with them. And earn with them. The *Whole Earth Catalog* is loaded with good earning ideas, survival ideas, machinery, and honesty. I'd consider the latest edition required reading for the economics of freedom.

There are supremely important little pieces of business knowledge floating around that you can learn by, again, dropping into your local library, reading trade magazines, talking to people who do it, writing to the U.S. government and asking for pamphlets on whatever you are attracted to, and just plain sitting down and thinking.

A few examples:

Some radio stations will let you advertise without your having to pay them *any* money. If you can interest a radio station in a particular product or service, yours or anyone else's, you can pay them on a P.O. basis.

P.O. stands for *per order.* And it means that for every person who orders (say, for $5) whatever you're advertising (say, a phonograph record), the station gets a percentage (say, $1) for every order you sent to them. They then keep their $1, send the $4 to you, and you pay $1.50 to the record company (your cost per record). Net profit to you: $2.50 per order. If you figure that each radio station will broadcast twenty-eight commercials a week (that's only four per day) and you know that they'll broadcast them only in unsold time (after midnight or before people awaken or some such) you will probably get a terrible response: maybe two orders per commercial.

But if you multiply 2 orders by 28 commercials, you get $140, figuring your profit at $2.50 per order. And if you multiply one radio station by ten radio stations, you get $1,400.00. Per week. *If* you know about P.O.

This whole thing required hardly any capital investment on your part. All you had to do was talk to the record-company person (letter, phone call, personal visit, contact), get him to sell you a $5.00 retail record for $1.50 in volume (no big problem), talk a radio station into selling you unsold time on a per order basis, be successful in a test run, and then mail enough letters to secure nine more radio stations to join in.

It's not nearly as easy as I just laid it out, but that's mainly because of Murphy. And games.

You can bring store owners together into merchants' associations. Just by bringing them together, you can enable them to promote their goods on a far more significant level than they could as individual stores. You can make money almost anywhere by this method, and after you've done the initial work, you have the freedom to continue helping them promote their stores (good money for you) or turn the whole thing over to an advertising agency (money for you). Try it on the commercial street nearest to where you live.

You can cut buying expenses like crazy while earning a bit on the side by forming your own co-op. Information on *how* to do this is in all libraries. You can form a co-op for food, clothes, cars, furniture, hardware, and more.

Look for growth communities. They're all over the world. You can go into automatic businesses—the kinds that automatically spring up and thrive: food, clothes, drugstore, restaurant, gas station, lots of others, too—and you can automatically prosper to a degree. Someone will. Why not you?

At this moment, you could make excellent money with

an employment agency in some towns, with a floral shop in others, with an auto-repair garage in some more, and with whatever in wherever. You *can* find out what and where by careful checking.

You can do your own specialized service for a specialized market, and advertise very inexpensively in a trade publication dedicated especially to people in this specialty. Just look up "Publishers—Periodical" in the Yellow Pages to get a line on what I'm getting at.

What you should understand is that you can *do* or *organize* ventures such as these. Many successful people had neither the ability nor the brains to succeed, but they surrounded themselves with the people who had these missing elements, and they succeeded in huge ways.

Your freedom to do or organize is a freedom possibly never afforded you before. But every work needs supervision and execution, and you may do either one or both or none in the economics of freedom.

In many cases, all you have to do is supply the idea, get the people who can do things together, and just be sure things run smoothly. And you can profit immensely and regularly from your effort.

Other times, you'll want to do the entire process all by yourself because you'll realize that you can handle a lot of details you've never handled before. Not because they were difficult. Only because they weren't available to handle.

Read the money-earning magazines, for inside are the keys to much knowledge. You'll get lots of ideas from magazines such as *Income Opportunities, Opportunity Magazine,* and the like. Check in any large magazine store and buy one of them. You'll get plugged into a whole world you may never have known existed. If you find any guaranteed opportunities in the magazine, take them up; really give them a try. Ads that guarantee things actually do guarantee them, but the advertisers know that few people avail themselves of their money-back privilege. Human nature. Nice to have knowledge of it.

Selling. Except for some salesmen, hardly anyone understands the true nature of selling, or the talent and consciousness needed for it. Yet it is the most available money-earning method around. Look in any major-market newspaper (there are about fifty major markets in the United States) and check the classified section for ads for salesmen or saleswomen.

In any economic situation, there is a crying need for good salesmen, with or without experience. Many sales opportunities require only part of your time.

If you can wrap your mind around the concept of *you selling,* you will become an automatic money earner. But first you've got to understand the nature of selling. And that's coming up in the next chapter.

There are several sources of the knowledge you'll need to successfully practice the economics of freedom. You'll find much of this knowledge in the Yellow Pages. You'll find even more in your local library. More still can be found in a good bookstore. Read the classified sections of newspapers for even more knowledge. While in your library, check a few editions (business publications, consumer magazines, radio) of SRDS (Standard Rate & Data Service).

These volumes will show exactly which media reach which people, how much it costs, and how to do it. In all likelihood, they'll open your mind to hundreds of opportunities you never before knew were around. They don't spell out the opportunities, but they give you the essentials you need to figure out the opportunities yourself.

While you're at the library, spend a little time reading

how people managed during the Depression of the early thirties. See which products and services thrived, then apply the principles to what is happening now. With a minor effort, you ought to be able to turn any bust into your own boom. And if enough join you, those in ranks of the unemployed might economically flourish again.

Other knowledge you'll need to function can be found by checking local regulations with regard to registering, licensing, and setting out a shingle to announce your work. Don't get involved in an innocent, yet profitable, pursuit only to learn that your community has hog-tied the pursuit with regulations.

Know this too: Most work is given to people who are connected to a grapevine. Sixty-five percent of job openings are not listed, for the same reason. If you're interested in a particular line of work (not a job, just work), plug yourself into the grapevine for that line of work.

To plug yourself in, just talk to and develop contacts among people who are doing the work. They'll reveal the grapevine, and you'll be privy to 65 percent more work opportunities than you are now.

In addition to the knowledge that appears in print, a lot comes to you when you combine two hitherto uncombined elements. For instance, many companies would love to give away free samples of their products, but it is just plain too expensive to waste samples on people who won't use them anyhow.

Related truth: Many people would love free samples of many companies' products. Put these two facts together and you can form a company that may be called something lofty like the Product Sample Council.

You can contact people to see how many want a year's worth of free samples, delivered once a month. You can charge them a tiny amount, say, $10 per year for twelve monthly deliveries of a slew of free samples. Fair.

You then can contact companies by mail, phone, or in person to see if they would like to distribute samples to people who have demonstrated that they want free samples. You can charge the companies a tiny amount, say, $2 per name. Fair.

You then can arrange for the companies to send the samples to you, and you distribute them to the people. Fair.

If you get one hundred people signed up for free samples (no big task with an inexpensive advertising program), that gives you $1,000. And if you deal with ten companies, each paying you $200, that's $2,000 more. With $3,000 and expenses of no more than $1,000, you stand to make a handsome before-tax profit just by putting together two pieces of knowledge that have never been combined before.

Again, I caution you that this example probably won't work out as easily in real life as in the pages of a book. But again it is because of Murphy. Though you possibly can make it work out if you always remember to ask the next question.

The next question—to be asked at almost every obstacle—is, Why not? Two words. Stick around until you get an answer and you'll be shocked at how much can be accomplished.

The economics of freedom allows, encourages, and suggests that you do as much yourself as you can. That doesn't mean that your earning time should eat into your unearning time. But it does mean that if you are earning via your own business, you should promote your business by yourself. At least at first.

Until you have enough to afford professional help, do your own public relations. All you have to do is talk to some newspaper people, interest them in running a story on your business because of some unique aspect—then keep up the relationship with the people by supplying interesting and newsworthy information on your company. Of course, there are four hard things connected with this suggestion:

1. It's hard to develop a good contact with a newspaper person so that he will take the time to listen to your story.
2. It's hard to be persistent enough to finally get the newspaper person in such a position that he becomes a potential contact.
3. It's hard to come up with an aspect of your business unique enough to justify a free newspaper story.
4. It's hard to repeat the above process with other newspaper people connected with other newspapers.

But public relations people get paid excellent money for doing just what I outlined—plus writing the story in the first place—and who knows? Perhaps you can accomplish the same thing, including the story (though a fact sheet is often enough; the newspaper people will write the story if you'd like). It certainly is worth trying while your business is new. And it doesn't cost a cent.

Try doing your own advertising as well. Talk to folks in related businesses in your community and see which advertising media work for them. Talk to the representatives of the media. Get their story. Then decide which media you'll use for initial advertising, and either write the ad yourself or get a modular writer and graphics expert to help you.

If you want to try other methods of promotion—distribute your own circulars, make your own phone calls, pay your own personal calls. After you're larger, you can delegate these responsibilities to others. But at first, do as much as you can yourself.

Knowing how to charge for what you make or do or sell also can have a profound effect upon your earnings. There is no set rule regarding this, but your business instinct should be attuned to the most propitious mode of charging at the moment. It varies with the times, the people, and the situations.

Naturally, large companies can afford to pay more than small companies—until the small companies become large companies due to your efforts. Naturally, it makes sense to charge more to companies that demand more of your time or more of your talent.

To know how best to charge means that you should know as many options as possible. You can charge by time: the hour, the day, week, month, or year. You can charge by the project.

There is a great deal of security in charging on a retainer basis—a set amount per month for an agreed-upon amount of work. You can charge on a percentage basis: percentage of sales, of profits, of increased business, of just about anything. I suggest you go for a percentage of gross sales. There's no ambiguity.

You also can work on commissions. The size of the commission is dependent solely upon the cost of the item being sold. You should expect about a 50 percent commission on an item sold to the mass market on a mass basis, such as cosmetics sold door to door. If you sell a $5 item, $2.50 is a fair commission for you.

On the other hand, if you sell someone's house for $100,000, a 3 percent commission would land you a neat

$3,000. Ordinarily, commissions are worked out by the organization that manufactures whatever is being sold. But as a guideline, figure that the costlier the item, the lower your commission.

Give careful thought to selling very high ticket items. If you sell just one million-dollar airplane, and earn just 1 percent per sale, you will need very few sales per year to put you into a lofty income bracket.

I seriously recommend that you work with your accountant in establishing commissions to charge for goods and for services. Only a trained accountant, or a similar business genius, can accurately figure costs per sale, selling and promotional budgets, and profit-and-loss statements—either your own or someone else's.

The business of business need not have any mystique surrounding it. But if you have been only a spectator at financial statements, I warn you against entering the arena as a participant. You need a money pro to help you past the mystique that has been created.

However you charge, or pay, or figure your monies, be sure that the important number upon which you focus is the profit.

Speaking of profits, you will learn that the word has no definition. If you do find a comfortable way to define the word, understand that you have succeeded academically, but failed financially. Profits are whatever the profiteer determines them to be. And that is very difficult for anyone to understand, including the profiteer.

My own accountant calls most financial record keeping "imaginative accounting." What he means is that the numbers you see are legal and honest, real and straightforward—but still they are not what they appear to be. They represent the careful and intelligent manipulation of assets and liabilities to a point that all but the most well-trained money people will be imaginatively hoodwinked.

Just because you are a novice at balance sheets and profit-and-loss statements does not mean you should ignore them. If you ever wish to obtain financing, bank assistance, or professional business aid, you will need these numerical records. So armed with a bright accountant, be prepared to present them: to the IRS, to a bank, to whomever is entitled to ask for them.

Incidentally, charge as much as you can to expenses—because you pay your taxes only on profits. Therefore, every cent you spent on your business that can possibly be labeled an expense should be treated as such. But resist the temptation to lie, pad your expenses, or call your ski trip a research trip—unless you are prepared to back your claim of research, and tie it in directly to your earning endeavor.

You will find untold opportunities for you to work "on the come." That means that you get paid nothing until the business succeeds. And then you get paid a lot. Since I have had both enjoyable and painful experiences working on the come, I can offer no advice on this matter. But I would like to meet someone who can. These days, I don't do it.

I suppose that until you have achieved your income goals, you should avoid gambling your time and energy. But after you have attained your aims, you can follow whatever your business instincts and feelings dictate. And sometimes they dictate that working on the come is proper.

You will earn more money if you do not allow your ego to interfere with your income. Pride is fine. But your ego must be flexible enough to accommodate difficult customers, discourteous clients, an abundance of negativism, unreasonable requests, insulting compensation offers, criticism, pseudo-expertise in your field by others, unreturned phone calls, unanswered letters, occasional disrespect, embarrassing questions, uninteresting detail work, and a host of other hassles that prove obstacles to success for others. Your income will rise in proportion to your ability to conquer these affronts to your ego.

Many of these behavioral bugaboos are concomitant to certain earning endeavors, and you must almost learn to expect them, just as blundering errors are an integral part of major league baseball.

Whenever I had been earning enough income, doing enough work, and achieving enough self-satisfaction, I said no thank you to new business that came my way. Upon looking back, I realize that I was wrong each time. I regretted each and every no thank you, and I now say yes thank you, then find a way to incorporate the new tasks at hand.

This may be considered greed at some times. But at other times it is more like survival. The point is that, unlike a job, which does provide a degree of security, earning without a job provides little security. Customers or clients are fickle, human, and woo-able by others. To protect yourself against their capriciousness, you need a few sources of income up your sleeve. You need a strong bench, as winning sports-team managers know.

Your bench strength will come from having more business than you need at the moment. And you'll be both surprised and dismayed to learn that more business than you need can instantly become barely enough business. So maintain a slight degree of paranoia, and welcome new business whenever possible.

In spite of the insecurity of intentional joblessness, if you really care about earning and earning until your earnings come out of your ears, you will find it simpler to earn more without a job than you can earn with a job.

Better still, you will soon develop a knack of doing it without spending too much time at it.

A good way to begin is, as I have indicated, to become beloved to your customers. This may be accomplished by always doing more than you are asked to do. Naturally, you should do what you are expected to do. Most people do that. But then they stop.

Not you, though. You should press on until you have done more than you contracted for, more than your customer or client expected, more than actually is necessary. If you and your customer have any disagreements as to how certain work is to be accomplished, a good rule to follow is to do it exactly as your customer requests. Then do it your way, too. Offer your customer the option. Whichever he chooses, you cannot help but be beloved. Appreciated. And called again for more work.

You should also do whatever is necessary to keep the ball in your client's court. That means that after you give your customer more than he bargained for, you should offer up a new idea that can lead to new work for you. Make it so the next step must be taken by the customer.

This can be done with a letter to your customer outlining a new project for yourself. A phone call can put the ball in his court. So can a memo, a sketch of future work, a rough outline, or an actual initiation of the first stages of the work you propose.

This forces the customer to take action, and makes you the focal point. It establishes you as a source of energy, ideas, and action. It is an automatic safeguard against the doldrums. If the customer owes you a reaction, you are far more likely to receive additional work than if he owes you nothing. The word that best describes this concept is *initiative.* You need a lot of it if you are determined to earn lots and lots of money. If you merely want to earn some money, you'll only need some initiative. Notice that there definitely is a correlation between initiative and income.

How will your customers feel about this initiative? Most

of them will love you for it. They'll feel impressed, appreciative, and confident. Nice things if you can get them. And you can get them if you try.

If your customers will pass the word around that you are a source of ideas and thought and action, constantly active, you will obviously be choosing to win by virtue of the initiative you put forth. And for it, you will deserve to win. Along with winning goes a remarkable shield against insecurity.

Speed. That's another thing you'll need to earn lots and lots of money. It's a pretty basic truth. And it's simple arithmetic. But too many people haven't figured it out yet.

It is possible to learn to work rapidly. It is even possible to work rapidly while exercising the same amount of conscientiousness that you do while working slowly. With few exceptions, almost every earning endeavor can be accomplished faster than most people now accomplish it. If you can work 33 percent faster, you should be able to earn 33 percent more. Twice as fast equals twice the income.

During my career, in almost any capacity, I knew that I was not the best at what I did. But I always was one of the fastest. Man, did that pay off.

Naturally, I always tried to improve, to become better. But I never sacrificed speed. Right now, almost everything that is done is done slower than necessary. Almost every book is longer than necessary. People have become numb to time. During your free moments, speed is unimportant, and slowness is probably a virtue. But during your earning hours, slowness is sinful.

I never miss a deadline. And yet I never get a speeding ticket. I consider that a good balance, and I recommend it if you wish to earn a lot of money and get a lot of enjoyment from life.

How can a piece of paper, a pen, and a cheap cassette tape recorder increase your income? Answer: by enabling you to record your good ideas. As you probably have learned from life, a good idea doesn't care when you get it, and doesn't confine its creation to your working hours. So keep a pen and paper near your bed, and on your person. And keep a cheap little cassette recorder in your car. This way, you won't forget any of your fleeting brainstorms. And all it takes is one great one to propel you into a higher tax bracket.

Just as important as having a lot of ideas is knowing the difference between the good and the bad ones. I think it is easier to get a lot of ideas than to judge them accurately. If you can do both, you ought to develop a close kinship with the large sums of money that should come your way.

Be unique.

That is especially crucial if you are in competition for your customers' dollars. If you wish to earn scads of money, you must do things to separate you from your competition. Doing the same work better and cheaper will help you, of course. But your competitors constantly will claim that they do it better and cheaper.

Therefore, you need to do it better and cheaper and then some. Your uniqueness can be offered in the form of more comprehensiveness, better service, more powerful advertising, an extra something or other, or possibly— your own personality.

You must offer whatever your competitors offer, and then you must offer even more. If your uniqueness takes the form of something extra for your customers, it will be a lot more meaningful and effective than a mere advertising or gimmicky uniqueness.

These days, people seem to have built-in bullshit detectors. That should prove a boon to you—especially if your uniqueness is an honest customer bonus.

You will also make more money if you can develop enthusiasm. Here's how to do it:

Realize that hardly anything is purely good or purely bad. Recognize the bad aspects of things, but concentrate upon the good. This is called positive perception. With enough positive perception, you can generate an honest enthusiasm for many things. It takes practice plus intelligence to perceive the positive in many things. But the more you look, the deeper you look, the more perspectives from which you look—that's how much positivity you will perceive. And the more you see, the more enthusiasm you will be able to develop.

Finally, with the ability to generate honest enthusiasm, you will find that you can sell better, perform better, communicate better, work better, deal with others better, and even compete better. Side benefit: It will make you a happier person.

But just because you become a positive perceiver does not mean that you should ignore the negative aspects. If you cannot change them, learn to live with and accept them. Ignoring them will not make them go away. So understand, then go beyond negativity.

You will also aid your earning capacity if you can constantly summon the guts to make decisions. The ability to make decisions is sadly lacking throughout the business world. Compared to the English, who are the worst decision makers I have ever encountered ("I mean maybe, and that's final"), Americans are great. Still, we have a long, long, long way to go.

If you have the courage to go out on a limb with a clear decision, you're already ahead of most corporate executives with whom I've come in contact.

Of course, you realize that I am saying you must risk being wrong. If you take the risk you will be wrong plenty of times. But you will also be right plenty of times. I see 51 percent as being a fairly healthy percentage of rightnesses over wrongnesses. And if you can maintain that kind of average, you'll do a lot better than those with no percentage at all. Most often, in a situation requiring a decision, you'll find no one who will be willing to decide. That keeps their percentage at 00 percent. Never wrong. Never right.

You will be much appreciated by many people if you are willing to be the person who makes the decision. Risking failure may not be their bag. So if you make it yours, you will achieve both failure and success.

A good way to earn lots of money is to know ways that save lots of money. Learning blacksmithing is such a way. It is probably the father trade because it enables you to make the tools for other trades.

With an anvil, a forge, a hammer, and a headful of blacksmithing prowess, you can make an enormous number of tools. Sure, you can sell them. You can also use them. You can rent them. You can repair them.

If you are to become the self-contained person who will flourish in the economics of freedom, blacksmithing will set you well on your way. Naturally, you can use your skills to make more than tools. But a person who can make the tools by which he will earn his keep will save more money, while keeping in close touch with grass-roots reality. Such experience will hone your business instincts as well.

Although you will possibly become engaged in several income pursuits, try to become an expert in each. This is not easy. But if you do it, you will earn more than if you do not do it.

If you are, for example, to have *anything* to do with flea markets, become a flea-market expert. It can make a big difference in how much you will earn from your flea-market endeavors. Shop several flea markets before you enter the business. Go to markets near and far from your home. Get there *before* they open, and stay until *after* they close. You will learn more from the opening and closing actions than from all the middles.

Read flea-market newspapers. Answer ads. Ask too many questions. Keep your pen and paper at the ready, for the notes you take will be your equivalent of a flea-market college education. You will be spending several weekends learning when you could be earning.

But what you learn will enable you to earn more during your first few months at flea marketeering than twice as many months spent without educational sojourns.

You will learn the whens, the whats, the whos, the hows, the wheres, and even the whys of flea markets if you visit a lot of them, and really check them out with intensity. After the initial hard work, you will dramatically increase your understanding, your fun, and your income. And then you'll be ready to develop the same degree of expertise in your other earning endeavors.

Again, it's not easy. But it can result in your earning an awful lot of money.

You also will earn more than your fair share of money if you engage in pursuits that automatically bring with them the opportunity for a lot of repeat business. If you decide to bronze baby shoes, you may attract many customers, but few will be repeat customers.

If you print and advertise address labels, your first customers will probably remain repeat customers for a long time. Selling and marketing greeting cards and matches are other pursuits with a great deal of repeat potential.

As a landscape architect, you will land several lucrative assignments. But once your creation is completed, your customers won't need your services anymore. They'll need a gardener instead. And the gardener will, if he or she is good, get all the repeat business. Naturally, you need not concentrate all your efforts in areas where repeat business is an attendant factor. But if you wish to earn like crazy, the more repeat business you get, the more money you will earn—and often, with little effort. And a lot of security.

Just as important as repeat business potential is mass-audience potential. Often, the two do not go hand in hand. You won't have to worry about repeat business if you can develop and market an item that will be purchased only once, but by every family in the nation.

To reach mass audiences, stay away from overspecialization. If you aluminize telescopic lenses, you may be compensated handsomely, but your services will not be in demand by a lot of people.

If you sell inexpensive felt-tip pens through gas stations, restaurants, drugstores, and groceries, you will be aiming smack-dab in the middle of the mass market. You can do the same by performing your service or selling your wares in bars, in offices, in public places.

One man made a fortune by inventing something that people would throw away. He felt that if he invented a long-lasting item, people would buy it and that would be that. So he invented razor blades instead. And King Gillette made a large fortune as a result. *Et tu?*

You will also make more if you specialize than if you do not. As much as can be said positively about specializing in one thing, even more can be said positively about specializing in many things. So whatever pursuits you follow, see if you can become a specialist in each.

Examples: If you are to be a traveling barber, try specializing in children's haircuts. It will give you a fierce competitive advantage; it will generate a lot of attention; it will call you to the attention of parents who wish to bring their shaggy kids to a children's haircutting specialist rather than a run-of-the-mill barber. If you're going to clean things, consider specializing in oil paintings. If you do, you will be one of the few. And a lot of people own oil paintings these days. Chances are, few of them know the first thing about cleaning their art. If you let your specialty be known, you just might find your services very much in demand.

If you become a mobile mechanic, you might do a lot better as a specialist in imported cars. By intimately knowing your sources of parts, and doing your homework on the cars you service, you probably will make out better than if you were a generalist.

So keep the thought of specializing in mind wherever your earning instincts take you. And consider having several specialties. It's difficult, but very effective.

You can earn lots of money if you are dishonest. And I hope that your dishonesty will cause this money to either be taken from you or to cease coming to you. Nonetheless, dishonesty is, although not the norm, all too accepted in the world of business.

Do not accept it yourself. Do not practice it either. It screws up the planet and also hurts your long-term earning possibilities. Regardless of your intelligence, your energy, and your ability, your reputation will become your most precious asset in time. If dishonesty is part of that reputation, it will be a deserved lifetime liability. And intelligence, energy, and ability will do little to overcome it.

You will frequently be tempted to bend honesty. You will see that if you do bend it, you will be in plentiful company. So leave the lack of ethics to the others. And let your inner nobility nourish your enthusiasm.

A great and honest businessman once told me (along with his other 799 employees) that the level of honesty in business is about equal or below the level of honesty in

politics. I believed him when he said these words because
I respected him. I believe him now because I have seen
the disregard of honesty on all levels of business. Not in all
business: only on all levels of business.

I have seen presidents of giant corporations knowingly
tell enormous and hurtful lies. But then, I also have seen
the President of my own country do the same. That he did
it was shameful, but not surprising. And if a man of his
official stature could be so blatantly dishonest, you can
expect corporation presidents—people of far less stature—to do the same. Not always. But sometimes. Not all
businessmen. But some businessmen.

Because you will often be forced to deal with the current economic system and its penchant for encouraging
tacky behavior, put your business arrangements in writing
whenever possible.

By writing a letter of agreement, and having your customer or client sign a copy, you will provide yourself with
protection. Certainly this letter will be no ironclad contract. But it should be enough to prevent you from being
exploited. Here is a typical letter of agreement that I use,
although the tone of the letter differs from customer to
customer:

Dear Robert:

It was both pleasurable and enlightening meeting with you and Michael. I'd be delighted to help
you achieve all of your business goals for Xxxxxxx. As
your Advertising Consultant, I would undertake responsibility for long-range advertising strategy, creative development of all advertising for all media,
supervision of all advertising, and direction of all
media efforts.

Graphics and production would be billed to you

directly, at my cost. Media buying and planning would be provided by one of the media-buying services with whom I deal. Actual media placement can be accomplished by them for you, or through your internal agency—which I will help you set up. Either way, you will not have to pay the standard 15 percent advertising agency commission.

My charge to direct all your communications efforts will be $1,000 per month for the first six months. After that, we will review my compensation in the light of workload and results achieved.

During that six-month period, I hope to give a fair trial to most media: newspapers to be sure, and magazines, too—along with radio and television. I will help you in the area of point-of-purchase signs and mailers to customers as a method of stimulating referral business.

My consulting fee will include all the work outlined above, plus one day per month in San Diego to meet with you. Naturally, I will always be available by phone or mail.

If we strike up a relationship, I will bill you on the fifteenth of each month, with payment requested for the first of the month following. In addition, a $500 start-up fee is required to commence the relationship.

Your plans seem realistic and ambitious, and I feel confident that I can help you attain your goals in an efficient and professional manner.

I ask for no contract, but hope that the relationship will continue as long as the results merit continuation. The relationship may be terminated by either party with 30 days' written notice.

Right now, I am looking forward to a long and

mutually rewarding association. Your check for $500 and your signature on a copy of this letter of agreement will put us in business. I eagerly anticipate working with you.

Optimistically,

_____

Jay Levinson
for Jay Levinson &
Partners

_____

Robert Meyerson
for Xxxxxxx, Inc.

I admit to losing in excess of $25,000, solely owing to my failure to get certain agreements in writing. Some of this total was lost even when I did have the agreement in writing. But I would have had to institute legal proceedings to collect. And I preferred to devote my energies elsewhere. I think time spent with lawyers is time subtracted from your stay in heaven.

This has been my problem. And I hope it does not become yours. I will do everything in my power to prevent myself from being further ripped off, yet I may find some of this effort futile. I promise, though, that I will get my agreements in writing. And if you don't, please don't say I didn't warn you right here and right now.

If I appear to be badmouthing the entire business community, I do not mean to do so. If I could mention the names of the people and the companies that I have personally witnessed in acts of overt dishonesty, and not run the risk of litigation, I joyfully would do so.

I fully realize that a great many businessmen (the majority, I hope, but I cannot be sure) are totally honest. The country is to be lauded to the skies for hounding a dishonest President from office. It spoke well for the honesty of the country that we could do this.

Still, whenever you can, get it in writing. As George Bernard Shaw pointed out, lack of money is the root of all evil.

There is a direct correlation between the size of your income and the openness of your mind. These days, more and more phenomena are being examined for rational explanation. ESP is being studied with more fervor than ever. Karate is proving that your thoughts can control your power.

I actually watched a man control gravity through sheer force of will, calling it the art/science of aikido. He stood between two strong men (Mike Connors, an actor, and Edgar Mitchell, an astronaut), then allowed himself to be lifted. Later, mustering all his aikido concentration, he stood between the same two strong men and could not be lifted from the floor. The two men strained honestly, but could not lift the lighter and smaller man. Thought controlled gravity.

Salamanders heal and regenerate better than any other creature. Why? Because of electricity of specific voltage and length that emanates from their brains.

People who can keep their minds open to such amazements can earn enormous sums of money if they can understand, develop, control, or otherwise goose evolution by harnessing these powers.

I have personally earned over $200,000 just because I kept my mind open to the concept of waterbeds, while other folks were poking fun or making sexual slurs with regard to this breakthrough in the relatively unknown science of sleep.

You will earn lots and lots of money if you define how much lots and lots really is, and you set monthly goals. Suppose you wish to earn $100,000 per year. That means you must earn $8,333.33 per month. Knowing that, you can begin to set targets.

Will you try for one $8,333.33 customer per month? Or might you more realistically aim for one hundred $83.33 customers? Can you make an $.83 monthly profit from ten thousand people? Or should you go for eight $1,041.67 customers?

The total income is up to you. The way you achieve it is up to you. But you should set monthly standards, so you know exactly what you are aiming for.

Perhaps $12,000 per year is lots and lots of money. This changes the mathematics drastically. And it may just be that you don't need lots and lots of money, and you wish to aim only for enough money. If $5,000 is enough, then $416.67 per month should be your standard.

The point is that if you will become goal-oriented with regard to income, you will become more successful at attaining your goal, and better able to determine along which earning avenues you will travel.

Keep your goals at peace with your energy level. And try to remember that money is only a means and never an end in itself. If you can agree with and comprehend this, dishonesty never will become part of your reputation. And your success will be measured by more than your income, regardless of its size.

CHAPTER
FIVE

Two Surefire
Money Earners

If you really want your freedom enough, you'll do the necessary homework and mind adjusting to become proficient in either or both of two nearly certain methods of earning money: selling and mail order.

Look through the classified section of any big-city Sunday newspaper. You'll find loads of selling jobs available. What is really available are selling opportunities. You won't have to take on a job to accomplish much of this selling. And you can contact many of the companies running help-wanted sales ads, only as a person interested in selling their product, and not as someone interested in a job. Watch: They'll be fascinated with your suggestion.

Look through most consumer monthly magazines—especially special-interest magazines. A plethora of mail-order ads beckon you to avail yourself of the convenience of purchasing an item via mail order. See? A whole lot of people have discovered that mail order *can* be a lovely source of income.

Of the thousands and thousands of ways to earn money, selling and mail order are so certain, so common, so increasingly popular, that it is worth devoting an entire chapter just to these topics.

Mind you, nothing is certain if you haven't laid the right foundation, or if you are attempting anything in a second-class manner. But with enough conscientiousness, selling and/or mail order can start you on your way toward the kind of life you envisioned when you purchased this book in the first place.

Some selling requires salesmanship. Some selling merely requires that you show or demonstrate the product or service you wish to sell, little else. All selling requires that you display confidence in what you are selling.

Salesmanship is something that certain people are born with. Yet it is something most people can learn. In order to sell something as a method of earning a living, you first have to make a conscious decision that you are going to sell.

This is very similar to making a conscious decision to quit smoking. Millions of smokers would like to quit smoking. But just wanting to quit isn't nearly enough. Some smokers actually arrive at a crucial moment when they make a clear, conscious decision to quit. It is those smokers—not all of them, but some—who are successful in quitting.

So too with selling. You can be successful to a degree with no sales talent if you have a good product, and many products do sell on sight.

But you can be wildly successful, financially and emotionally, if you decide that you are going to sell, to sell well, and to love selling. If you truly believe that you're going to enjoy selling and succeed at selling, you're 75 percent home.

Just what do you sell? Well, almost anything. But since

this book deals with total freedom for you, that consideration will guide you in selecting just what you do sell. It might be a good idea to study your own list of credentials and interests before deciding exactly what you sell. If you've spent most of your life working in a factory, you may be at a loss when it comes to selling cosmetics door to door. But you may be a whiz at selling to industry. On the other hand, if you've been a housewife most of your life, you may be a whiz at selling those cosmetics. The options are yours.

If you make up your mind to be good at selling, take yourself to your local library and check out a few books on salesmanship. If you can get your hands on some tape-cassette sales-training courses, listen to them, for they are worth far more than their weight in gold. There are some excellent books on the subject of selling (see appendix). And if you know what is in them *and* you have the honest desire to succeed at selling, there is hardly anything that can stop you.

If you've never sold before, consider that an advantage—and let your product do the selling for you. Be honest enough to admit your lack of sales experience and turn your customers' attention to the product. If you are careful in selecting the product and the potential customers, it is true that you may only have to show the product to sell it. If you sell by that method, you are an order taker. Order takers have a relatively easy life, but make considerably less money than salesmen.

Know that one of our natural quirks is to want to be sold. So if your customers show little interest in what you have to sell, try selling them and watch how many of them buy. It is easier to do than to explain.

One of the nicest things about selling is that everyone is a potential customer for something. And you get to pick out the items and the customers. You can sell to stores, offices, factories, homes, shoppers, motorists, doctors, dentists, students, housewives, commuters, gas stations, newspapers, motels, and more.

You can sell things by yourself, or you can merely select items and organize a group of commissioned salespeople to sell for you. The economics of freedom permits this. But if you're not going to do the sales job yourself, be sure to train your commissioned salespeople how to sell.

I conduct sales training for three of my clients. And I must admit that I am better at sales training than at sales. Still, I have sold innumerable things, from ladies' shoes to Fuller brushes to men's shirts to kitchen tables to waterbeds to whiskey—and I know that selling is a vastly underestimated method of earning money.

Work is always available. You can earn money as you learn. You can earn money even if you're lousy at first. It is work that virtually anyone can do. And you can handpick what it is that you will sell.

The entire selling system has joys that are reserved for it and it alone. The idea of hiring a selling organization to sell your wares and doing it with less than a $100 capital investment is a heady thought indeed. But you can do it because salespeople do not need a salary; commission only will do it. In fact, anyone who has made a conscious decision to *sell* will want to work on a commission-only basis. More money for them; less capital expenditure for you. Everyone gains: a lovely side effect in the economics of freedom.

Once you decide to sell, don't try to go it alone: Use sales aids, for they can make an immense difference. If you can demonstrate what you are selling, that, too, makes a difference. And if you can show pictures of the benefits or results of buying what you are selling—what you are saying to your customers will become 68 percent more meaningful.

Studies do prove that a visual representation of a verbal communication does increase comprehension by 68 percent. So ask for or create your own sales aids. The professionally produced aids are the best, and they ordinarily are supplied free to the salesperson.

You don't even need a sample of your wares; a catalog will do. Catalogs of certain types of jewelry are readily available from manufacturers (find their names in *Income Opportunities* magazine), along with sales aids. All you've got to do is show the catalog, use the sales aids, and write up orders. And that's just one example of many. You can do the same with seed catalogs, furniture catalogs, and catalogs of endless other kinds of merchandise.

As a general rule, it makes good sense to sell proven items rather than new items—especially if the items have been proven in other towns and aren't yet available or offered in your town.

You can sell crime-prevention devices. Some of these are available to you for $.80 and retail for $2.95. You pocket the difference. All you need to purchase is one $.80 item, and that's your entire capital investment. That, plus any sales aids you wish to make, buy, or borrow.

But don't limit yourself to proven items. New inventions can make you rich, if they're good enough. I know one man who sold waterbeds from a catalog to motel owners at a popular vacation area. He made big money because the motel owners needed a competitive edge, and the waterbeds did it for them. Once they listed waterbeds on their marquees, their business increased to the point that many other motel owners were forced to install waterbeds as well. And wasn't my friend happy? He made as much in three months as many people do in a year. And to date, most vacation areas are untapped with regard to waterbeds.

That's just one relatively new invention that can earn money for you.

Just the opposite are antiques. You can check with antique stores to see what they want or need, and then you can shop the flea markets and swap meets to purchase and sell what the stores requested.

You can place a few tiny classified ads asking for antiques on consignment. You can sell these at flea markets yourself and keep the markup all to yourself. In one day you can earn enough to last a week. And your capital expense is the rental of a flea-market stall plus the cost of a few small classified ads.

Does this qualify as selling? Of course it does.

You can sell industrial maintenance products at your old factory or to any other factory, for that matter. You can join the ranks of thousands who earn handsome livings selling advertising specialties on a part-time basis.

Advertising specialities are imprinted (with the name of a business) on pens, pencils, calendars, booklets, ashtrays, lighters, desk ornaments, phonebook covers, novelty items, and enough other doodads to fill a 568-page catalog.

You can sell Bibles. You can sell Fuller brushes. You can sell encyclopedias. You can sell Avon cosmetics. You can sell almost anything anywhere: door to door, office to office, or store to store. You can even sell lakes and mountains.

You can develop your own leads or you can sell items for people who supply you with leads. Take encyclopedias or pots and pans. Manufacturers of these items advertise, and frequently feature a coupon in their ad. People become interested in the ad and return the coupon, requesting more information.

Enter you—armed with more information, armed with sales aids, armed with samples, and armed with your conscious desire to *sell*. Best of all, you are now confronted with someone who wants to *buy*. Congratulations to both of you.

An insurance salesman loves to make sales calls in groups of nine because statistics have proved to him that for every nine calls he makes, he'll make one sale. So if he calls on ten groups of nine (calling upon the people one at a time), he'll make ten sales.

And so it goes for all selling. In time, you'll know how many sales calls you have to make in order to close one sale. And the name of the game from that point on is to increase the ratio of sales to number of calls, and to increase the number of calls. Simple arithmetic. And it adds up to money for you.

Of all the ideas with which you will be confronted in these pages, selling is probably the most lucrative, the most available, and the most permanent. This coming Sunday, check the help-wanted section of the biggest newspaper you can find, and see how many sales jobs are offered. Don't forget, though, you don't want a sales job; you want sales work. The difference is enormous.

Another point to keep in mind: Selling, mail order, and just about everything else in life all have a common denominator. It is *doing all aspects right*. If you do everything right except for one teeny thing, everything may come out wrong for you.

If a baseball team has power, speed, fielding, intelligence, and cohesiveness, but lacks pitching, that team will most likely win no pennants.

There is a retail furniture and appliance store in Edmonton, Alberta, in Canada. Word got out that this store was selling about ten times as much as similar-sized stores in the United States. What was the secret?

Two friends of mine journeyed to Edmonton to find out. They examined every possible reason for the incredible success of the store, looking for the hidden secret. The secret turned out to be no secret at all: The store was doing all aspects of its business right. There were no weak links. Every single facet of the business was run as superbly as it possibly could be run. Major items like sales and advertising were as smooth and professional as customer service and accounting. By doing absolutely everything as perfectly as possible, the store was (and is) enjoying phenomenal success.

Selling and mail order might tend to sound a bit easier on paper than they are in real life. You've got to handle every aspect of them with total professionalism in order to make these endeavors pay off for you. Nothing mysterious about it. Yet few people have the comprehensive conscientiousness to pull it off.

In order to succeed at mail order, you need: (1) the right product, (2) the right ad, (3) the right media. An immense number of people are cashing in on the sixty-billion-dollar mail-order industry every day. And to start, many of them had well under $1,000. With more, you have as good a chance as many current millionaires, provided you have the right knowledge and the right instincts. And even if you don't have them now, you can develop the instincts and gain the knowledge. The instincts aren't for sale. But the knowledge is (*Direct Mail and Mail Order Handbook*, $32.50 from Dartnell, 4660 Ravenswood Avenue, Chicago, Illinois 60640).

Mail order (and direct mail) is a business that anyone can start, that may be accomplished from home, that never requires full-time effort (unless you so desire), that gives you independence and freedom, and that can result in a steady income for life.

The differences between direct mail and mail order are minimal. Mail order is an advertisement in a publication (or on radio or TV) for an item that people order by mail or phone. The skills required for success are ability to select a product, ability to write an ad, and ability to select the right media for running the ad. Direct mail is a letter and/or brochure mailed to people who order the item by mail or phone. The skills required for success are ability to select a product, ability to write a letter and/or brochure, and ability to select the right list of people (obtained from a list broker) to whom you mail the letter and/or brochure.

It is even possible to enter the direct mail and mail-order field with none of these skills. They can be supplied for you (Mail Order Associates, 120 Chestnut Ridge Road, Montvale, New Jersey 07645; $75).

However you enter the business, here's approximately how it works. You spend $30, for example, to run an ad for a product. Twenty people send you $5 each to buy what you advertise. The cost of what you are advertising is $2 to you. So you have spent $70 of your own money ($30 for the ad plus $40 for twenty $2 items) and you have collected $100. If your postage and handling costs are $5, your total profit is $25.

Not a lot of money, to be sure. But suppose you ran the ad in ten different publications per week. Then your profit is $250 per week. And if you can obtain results like that, you might try one hundred different publications, with a projectable profit of $2,500 per week. The results can be outstanding—*if* you have the right product, message, and medium.

Working with a company like Mail Order Associates, or

several others who offer similar deals, you need not ever invest the money for the product, pay postage, or handle shipping. They do that for you. All you do is select the product, invest in advertising it (your ad or theirs), and collect the profits, if any. Because you can start with so little, and end up with so much, mail order is definitely worth looking into as an adjunct earning endeavor to anything else you may do.

I have been a professional advertising person for over thirty years with a high degree of expertise in writing advertising, and far more than an average knowledge of media. Because I have created advertising for items and services of all kinds, and because I have seen the results of literally millions of dollars' worth of consumer research, I have developed a well-tuned sensitivity to the public's tastes. Armed with these impressive qualifications, I seem to have everything it takes to succeed at mail order.

But I haven't succeeded in any big way. I am quite a bit past the break-even point, but I sure haven't come anywhere near making the fortune that many one-man enterprises claim. Worse yet, I'm not sure whether I've been separated from success by my poor choice of products, my poor advertising writing, or my poor media instincts. I suspect that I am a better writer and media selector than product selector, so perhaps it is because I haven't yet come up with the right product.

But I'm still trying. I still get excited over the possibility of making over $500,000 with one ad in one magazine—such as happened to a mail-order person in Vermont, whose ad in *Sports Afield* magazine resulted in 22,000 orders—or the countless one-person mail-order companies that report sales of up to $100,000 per year.

I know that the possibility does exist, and I'm going to keep on trying. If you do, I wish you more success than I've achieved.

Incidentally, the most painless way of entering the mail-order field is through a company that will supply catalogs of mail-order items to you along with ads for the catalog or items, and ask that you pay nothing for goods until they are ordered. These companies handle all the details for you, and all you have to do is purchase lists and mail the catalogs to the names, or run pre-created ads for the catalogs, and mail one to each person who orders. Ads by many such companies can be found in *Income Opportunities* magazine and others of that ilk.

A more exciting, though perilous, method of going the mail-order route is by advertising your own thing. In my case, I have written brochures for and advertised books that I have written. Others do it with food (candy, short-bread, other nonperishable-in-a-hurry items), with recipes, with imported goods, with hand-painted T-shirts, and with just about anything.

The money-opportunity magazines are brimming with ads by companies that give you your choice of dozens of fancy imported items to sell by mail order. Many of these companies will sell you items at wholesale, will obtain items that you couldn't get through ordinary channels, will drop-ship for you (that means you send them the order once you receive it from a respondent to your ad, and they ship it for you), will supply you with a list of names already on gummed labels (all you have to do is send catalogs or direct-mail pieces to the names), and will provide you with items that are proven mail-order winners.

With so much offered to people, it's a wonder everyone isn't in the mail-order business. Example: There's a company that will (1) show you where to get names of recent new mothers, and (2) supply you with catalogs of baby items. All you've got to do is send the catalog to the mother, then get ready to open envelopes and deposit checks. The company will handle all the rest. It sounds so very simple, I wonder what the world is waiting for.

The point of all this is that although mail order is beautifully tempting, it is a field that is loaded with competitors, and is probably more complex than you think. If you decide to try it, by all means check the books in your library and bookstore first. There are a lot. Don't expect to gain results with one ad. And have enough capital to test several products. And ads. And media. But if you do come up with the right combination, you might find that the economics of freedom will provide you with six free days per week, and plenty of money to spend all six days. Good luck.

Along with my wishes of luck, I reiterate my recommendation of the book *How You Too Can Make at Least $1 Million (But Probably Much More) in the Mail-Order Business* by Gerardo Joffe.

Mr. Joffe unquestionably has succeeded where I have not. He not only runs a delightfully successful mail-order company, but has already sold two mail-order companies to nationally known corporations for several million dollars. He has a knack for starting a mail-order company, then selling it to another national corporation for even more millions of dollars.

How does he do it? Same way the Edmonton store does it—by doing everything right.

Of course, there is a science to selecting the right product. Mr. Joffee reveals the source of that science. He tells you where to find unique mail-order merchandise: foreign trade publications such as *The Importer*, c/o East Asia Publishing Company, 2-11 Jingumae, 1-Chome, Shibuyaku, Tokyo 150, Japan ($20 per year); *Hong Kong Enterprise*, 3rd Floor, Connaught Centre, Central Hong

Kong ($20 per year); *Asian Sources,* c/o Trade Media Ltd.,
P.O. Box K-1786, Kowloon Central, Hong Kong ($25 per
year); *Made in Europe,* P.O. Box 174027, D-6 Frankfurt/
Main, 17, West Germany ($30 per year); and America's
great mail-order source, *Direct Marketing,* c/o Hoke Publications, 224 7th Street, Garden City, New York 11535
($24 per year).

Here you will find items that are not generally available in the United States. You might find products that are
advertised to do one thing, but that can be repositioned
to do another.

To select the proper items for mail order, develop one
or more promotional items and compile a list of proven
buyers. Select a niche for your mail-order company, then
offer items that fill that niche. The niche may be fishing,
or carpentry, or outdoor living, or plants, or just about
anything.

Continue looking for items to broaden your offering.
You'll find these items not only in the publications I just
listed, but also at trade fairs, in competitors' catalogs, and
in both consumer and trade publications.

Be sure you price your merchandise properly. There
are many formulas put forward for pricing. Study several
of them, and don't forget, the name of your game is profitability.

Do everything you can to make your products
unique—through naming, packaging, designing, and everything else you can think of.

Once you have a list of folks who have bought from you,
once you have a list of proven mail-order items, and once
you have been in business long enough to consider your-

self somewhat of an expert in mail order and direct mail, it is time to give thought to publishing your own catalog. This is where mail order *really* begins to pay off.

Some mail-order pros feel you are not completely into the mail-order business until you have a catalog. Certainly it is more complicated to develop a catalog than a mere ad, but the payoff is well worth it, according to most mail-order mavens.

Along with a catalog, by the time you develop one, you should have developed proficiency at businesslike skills such as inventory control, data processing, customer service, and record keeping. Accurate record keeping is one of the keys to success in direct marketing.

You've probably heard of people who have run successful mail-order companies working from their kitchen table. Is this really true?

It sure is. You can begin, and even begin to prosper, from your kitchen table. But eventually, you'll need more room, more tables, and maybe even your own building.

In a book such as this, there is a natural tendency to oversimplify certain businesses. Without that tendency, this book could run to several thousand pages. Therefore, I am forced to leave out details, even important details. But I strongly suggest that you go from this book to books that deal directly with the fields in which you select to earn.

A book devoted entirely to mail order goes into all the necessary details. And regardless of how you are going to earn money without a job, I remind you to use this book only as a springboard.

Example: One book on mail order tells you to have $5,000 to $10,000 available—either by yourself or through a relationship with a bank. It details the arrangements you should have with your bank, attorney, accountant, insurance man, and yourself. It discusses the importance of your company name, the line of merchandise you offer, the crucial significance of customer service. Of course, it deals with advertising, the need to accept credit cards, the inadvisability of mail-order courses, and mailing preexisting catalogs. It discusses the problems and opportunities of buying a going mail-order business, and it lays out enough home truths to enable you to decide clearly whether or not the mail-order business is right for you.

Don't forget: Unless you accomplish all aspects of the business right, it will not work well.

Nonetheless, in the economics of freedom, an income from a mail-order company can be long-lasting, substantial, consistent, growing, forever welcome, and not very demanding of your time—once you have it coming in. So whatever you consider as earning endeavors, you should consider them in terms of mail order, if at all possible.

To make it in most nonjob earning activities, you have to be able to delegate. In the mail-order business, if you have a talent for selecting the right products, you can delegate the ad writing and the media or list selection.

On the other hand, you can be a lead-pipe cinch for success in the mail-order and direct-mail business if you have the following fourteen things going for you:

1. An ability to organize your work and your time.
2. An ability to stand up under pressure and frustrations, to bounce back.
3. An ability to get along with people or, mainly, radiate a lot of empathy.
4. An elementary knowledge of ordinary business procedures: typing, filing, bookkeeping, record keeping.
5. An affinity for timeliness, an inclination to keep abreast of the times.

6. A talent for generating ideas.
7. A command of the language so that you can conduct business correspondence.
8. A "radar" for merchandise selection.
9. An inclination toward inventiveness—especially toward something you can invent (cook, write, create, construct) and then sell.
10. Artistic ability that can be directed toward producing your own artwork for ads and catalogs.
11. An ability to write convincing, believable, and persuasive copy.
12. A way with numbers and a penchant for analyzing data, plus an ability to evaluate results and project costs, sales, and profits.
13. Knowledge of business management, accounting, control systems.
14. A desire to earn money without a job.

Although there is a close relationship between mail order and direct mail, to the astute person in the direct-response business, there is a world of difference.

Ideally, your mail-order business goes well enough for you to compile a list of satisfied customers. That list, at the very minimum, should be 100,000 names long. The harvesting of these names is a method by which you can get into the really lucrative part of the business.

You harvest the names with direct-mail pieces, with package inserts, and with catalogs. Earlier I said that you need the right product, the right ad, and the right list to succeed at direct mail. With 100,000 satisfied customers, you are 33 percent home.

By careful determination of why these people bought in the first place, and what they bought, you ought to have little trouble selecting the right product and the words necessary to sell the product. So let direct mail come a bit after mail order is going well for you.

An incidental joy that comes with the successful development of a mail-order business is that it is quite a salable commodity if it has a good record of profitability.

Large corporations don't want to take the time to test and experiment with mail-order marketing, but they are more than happy to consider the purchase of a company that already has undergone all the testing and experimentation.

If you can generate profits from your mail-order company for, say, five years, you can seriously consider selling it for a gigantic sum to a gigantic company.

Selecting products, writing promotional propaganda, and choosing media or lists is a lot more fun than keeping accurate records and running close controls on your inventory and profits. If the business ceases to be a source of happiness, you should think seriously about selling it. If you do sell it, you can start all over again if you wish, and sell another. Or you can plop yourself down in your favorite plop spot, and live off the interest from your company sale price.

As you continue with this book, you will learn of many ways to earn. But at this point, you should realize that hardly any single way offers as good a chance for planned success as mail-order—hardly any will allow you such a huge payoff, and hardly any can be built with as much expectation of achieving your goals.

You *must* do all the aspects of it correctly. You must understand that there are no guarantees or sure things, no magic formulas or hidden secrets—but with hard work and decent instincts, you can gain all the freedom, income, and satisfaction you wish, from just a few well-spent years in the mail-order business.

Best of all, that business is still in its infancy. It has a long way to go; it is constantly growing; and there is plenty of room for new mail-order businesses. Even more, you can begin while still employed.

Selling is not easy. Mail order is not easy. Earning money without a job is not easy. But as far as I'm concerned, they're all a whole lot easier than working at a boring job with a limit to your success and an automatic curtailment of your freedom.

CHAPTER
SIX

No Capital Needed

Ask almost anyone and you'll hear that it is absolutely impossible to earn money with your own business unless you have sufficient capital.

Not true.

What is true is that the more capital you have, the greater are your chances for success. But there are zillions of money-earning possibilities that require little or no capital. I started my business with no capital. Four of my current clients (owners of sizable businesses) started their companies with no capital. And the world is loaded with millionaires who began on a shoestring, and a ratty old torn shoestring at that.

In this chapter, you'll learn of a slew of money-earning methods that require no more than $100 to get started.

It's true that some of these avenues will require a little more money. But do not worry: You can amass that money while you're working, and you'll need less than $100 to begin.

As you allow the earning possibilities listed in the following pages to filter through your mind, recognize that some of them probably will not lead you to a large amount of money, while others may well bring you a big, beautiful bundle of cash.

The degree of success in these money earners is very much up to you. If you decide to baby-sit, you probably won't make a lot. But if you start a baby-sitting service that becomes the largest and busiest in your town, you might make enough to spread to other towns—which might end up making you the state's wealthiest baby-sitter.

The amount of time you devote to earning, your ability to delegate, your desire to expand—these factors will influence how much you can make. In nearly every case, the idea put forth has the outside possibility of earning a small fortune for you—merely by intelligent delegation of responsibility, promotion of the service, and ability to expand into other markets. Of course, some earning ideas suggested are not delegatable, promotable, or expandable. But how much you earn from these endeavors is really up to you.

The more of these ideas that you pursue, the less time you will have to devote to any single idea. If I were you, and I probably am, I would attempt several of these endeavors, then concentrate on the most financially lucrative and emotionally satisfying.

To gain more information about these upcoming ideas, you'll have to be creative. In some cases, the bibliography in the appendix will help. In other instances, a visit to your local bookstore or library will be in order. The federal government may be able to supply some information about other concepts advanced here.

But for the most part, there will have to be a lot of free-lance fact finding on your own part. You will find nothing in print about installing tire chains, or being a live-in, and on these and most of the other ideas you will have to get information by asking around, by using your good old horse sense, or simply by doing. Don't let this lack of formal information set you back. Instead, look upon it as an opportunity for *you* to write the definitive piece on the subject. It is crucial that you understand that this chapter, this book, and this economic system are all predicated upon your own ability to get ideas. The ideas put forth here are enough to earn loads of money for you, and to keep you busy with work from now till you're retired to the old folks' home. Still, these are but a small sampling of the many ways you may earn money practicing the economics of freedom. Future editions of this book may include many new ways suggested in letters from you. And no book, regardless of how advanced the edition, can come close to listing *all* the ways there are to earn money.

But for starters, try any one, two, three, or ten of these.

Read a Magazine

To repeat what I have already repeated, read some of the money-opportunity magazines. Take up some of the offers. Don't be hoodwinked by fancy promises, and protect your interests. But there's gold in them there pages, and a job isn't required to strike it.

Raise Consciousness

Take almost anything that you know well. Then spread the word. Perhaps you can teach salesmanship; almost any retail store needs help in that area. If you can teach the fundamentals of something and raise the consciousness of the students to accept using the fundamentals, you can make a lot of money for the students, for your customers, and for yourself.

Sit Somewhere

Baby-sit. Advertise that you do it. Or organize a team of baby-sitters and advertise that *they* do it. It's a continuing need and one that can earn you money right now— tonight.

Wash a Window

Invest in a long-handled squeegee, a pail, and a good glass cleaner. *Voilà!* You are in the window-cleaning business. Go from store to store offering to wash windows and you'll be amazed at how many acceptances you get. Print up business cards and get ready for a lot of repeat business.

Be a Homebody

Be homey. But not in your own home—in someone else's. Offer to perform any of the work necessary in a home: oven cleaning, floor washing, wall washing, dishwashing, vacuuming, ironing, everything. You can pick the days you work, and your capital investment is minimal, since the home probably will have all the necessary equipment.

Walk on the Beach

Collect driftwood. Collect shells. Collect rocks. Collect sand. Somewhere someone wants to buy driftwood, shells, rocks, and sand. Find out who wants to buy, then go take your walk on the beach.

Board a Boat

Go down to the nearest boatyard and offer your services. Offer to wash, scrape, paint, varnish, sand, clean, or whatever else they may need. They'll need something and you'll earn money as a result. I promise you that if you had been at the boatyard where I keep my boat, you would have been offered a lucrative fee to give it a going-over last Sunday.

Smoke a Fish

During fishing season, just wait where the fishermen return. For well under $100, you can own a smoker of your own and, for a few cents more, you can letter a sign saying "Fish Smoked Here." Chances are, you'd catch your limit of fishermen every weekend, and you'd pick up some decent money besides. Smoking fish is an easy skill to learn.

Raise a Worm

Out near where I live, there's a man who makes over $100,000 a year just raising worms, which he sells to fishermen, bait shops, and organic gardeners. Once you've done the preliminary soil conditioning, the worms do most of the work. Just be sure you check with bait shops and gardening stores before embarking upon this venture—to ascertain a demand for your supply. And the demand is growing as organic gardening increases.

Start a Flea Market

It's easy. Find the land—it doesn't have to be expensive. Rent it for a weekend, and put up notices on bulletin boards and in classified-ad sections of local papers. Invite stall holders and ordinary people to sell their wares at your place on your selected date. Soon word will get around (especially if you offer neat things at your flea market in the way of items, food, and entertainment), and you will be able to operate every weekend, weather allowing. You make your money by charging either a percentage of each stall holder's take or a flat fee. Let the world know of your market via word of mouth, bulletins on supermarket and other community boards, classified ads in flea-market newspapers, and tasty signs posted nearby. Your location can be far from a populated area if it is near a restaurant or recreation area.

Stand at a Stall

Operate your own stall at a flea market. Make it yourself and stock it with anything. Anything? Anything. Almost everything you own is of value to someone, so offer things for sale: old clothes, books, records, doodads. Take goods on consignment from others. (You pay them only after you've sold what they want you to sell, and you have taken your fair percentage.) Unlimited freedom in what you are selling is yours at a flea market. I know a woman who makes a week's worth of money just selling homemade food and drink at weekend flea markets. I know another who averages $100 in profits per day. Lovely.

Help a Going Business

Many going businesses need to expand but don't know how. You can help a store immeasurably if you offer to start a direct-mail program, mail-order program, door-to-door program, or party-plan sales program for them. They've got the name, the merchandise, the reputation, the advertising. Only they haven't got the time to expand into these areas. So they'll appreciate you for giving them the opportunity. Think of which stores would most benefit from such an effort, then talk to their owners. Example:

A man who owned a plant store was approached by an economics-of-freedom practitioner who asked to represent the plant store at offices. Offer accepted. Profit realized by both. Example: A boutique never sold at night, never had a direct-mail program. A smart woman talked the proprietor into trying both: a direct-mail invitation to a nighttime sale. Result? Exceptional. The opportunities are always there. The time to spot them is now. Someone will. Why not you?

Teach a Class

Whatever you know well, someone else might want to know well, too. While I was working at a full-time job in an advertising agency and I was in my late twenties, I earned money teaching advertising one night per week. I taught students in their teens who knew a lot less than I. What can you teach? Cooking? Welding? Car repair? Computers? Art? Fishing? Sewing? Plumbing? Painting? Wallpapering? Gardening? Electrical maintenance? Camping-out techniques? Tennis? Swimming? Whatever, you can teach at your home, in a store, in a rented building, at a community college, in an adult education center, or in a cooperative venture with other people teaching other things. You can make pretty good money: $25 per student for a six-week course will net you—with, say, 15 students—$375 for six evenings over the course of six weeks. Not bad. Double it if you teach two courses.

Hold a Garage Sale

Hold your own garage sale to raise a little money. But to raise a lot of money, hold garage sales for others. In return for your organizing the sale, your promoting the sale, your handling the sale, and your doing the actual selling (really order taking), you are entitled to about 10 to 40 percent of the total take. Once you develop a reputation for successful garage sales (no great talent needed), you'll get called in to handle sales where up to $3,000 changes hands in a day. Your slice of that is $300. Maybe even $1,200. Not bad for one day's work. And these days, many people who never held a garage sale would like to hold one. So what are you waiting for?

Be a Temp

You can't make a permanent career out of being a temporary employee, and you probably wouldn't want to anyway. But you can earn money as a temp without holding a job, and you probably can get temporary work in a hurry if you'd like. Just check the classified ads under Help Wanted, or call some employment agencies that specialize in temps. If special skills are required, learn a few—and you'll be able to temp your way through an economic crunch while maintaining your freedom.

Latch on to a Grant

Every year, millions and millions and millions of dollars are being given away in grants to deserving people. Check your local library to see how you can become deserving. Check also on the fields in which grants are given. Perhaps, with a little help, you can put together the requirements to qualify. In truth, millions of dollars are not given away just because no one asks for or qualifies for certain grants. It's becoming so complex that some people now earn a living as a grant consultant. I couldn't find any in the Yellow Pages, but if you talk to a few grant-giving organizations, they'll probably be able to direct you to a helpful soul.

Advertise a House

Check the classified section of the Sunday paper and see which real estate ads are the most poorly written. Offer to write the want ads for a realtor (if you can do better) and collect a fee for each house he sells. Many of the house ads running these days are terrible; most of the others sound alike. Just by being different, or warm, or humorous your want ad can sound more appealing than others. And both you and your realtor can cash in handsomely.

Pen a Column

Write a regular column for a small local newspaper. The column will be successful if it has local gossip, names, people's travel plans, special pets, unique hobbies, and/or achievements attained. The local newspaper will pay a small but fair price, and by keeping your ears open and writing proper English, you can put some extra cash into your coffers. And maybe even win a Pulitzer Prize.

Hook on to a Cable

Get to know the people at your local cable TV outlet. You can earn money through them if you attract an advertiser. Just convince any local merchant to spend a few dollars advertising on local cable TV, and you can get a small, regular check in return. Convince three local merchants and you can get a medium, regular check in return. Idea: Talk to a real estate broker. If she runs a one-minute commercial on cable TV, and shows six houses in the commercial, for ten seconds each, she'll get a lot of house hunters watching her commercials, she'll attract a lot of house sellers to her (because who else can offer them TV coverage of their house?), and she'll sell a lot of houses as a result. As for you, if you do well with your local cable TV outlet, you can expand to all the other cable TV outlets in your region. And collect a lot of regular checks.

Sell a Sandwich

I paid for at least one semester of college by selling sandwiches at places where people could not otherwise buy them. I arranged with a local eatery to make a dozen ham sandwiches, a dozen beef sandwiches, a dozen cheese sandwiches, and a dozen meatball sandwiches (the eatery specialized in meatball sandwiches). I collected the forty-eight sandwiches, brought them to fraternity houses, sorority houses, and dormitories, and hollered out (at about nine P.M.) "Sandwiches! Ice cream! Milk!" I sold all forty-eight sandwiches (for exactly twice what I paid for them) plus the ice cream and milk in about one hour. I only worked two nights a week, but I earned enough for one expensive semester. Working seven nights a week, you can make a small fortune. And your days will be free. The concept here is to offer sandwiches (food) where sandwiches (food) are not ordinarily available. Likely places would be apartment buildings, dormitories, factories, in front of schools, at beaches, at demonstrations, and in parks on weekends. You can increase your profits dramatically if you also make the sandwiches. Check with your local board of health to see what regulations you must comply with.

Make a Boot

One day, my wife and I received a phone call from a man who said he was given our name by a mutual friend. Said he was in the neighborhood and he'd like to show us some very inexpensive custom-made boots and shoes. Since I had never heard of such a thing, since the time was 8:30 P.M. or something, since nothing special was on TV or happening in the house, and since my wife had always told me she wanted the luxury of custom-made boots, I invited the gentleman over. He arrived with boots, shoes, and juicer. After wooing us with a weird vegetable-juice concoction that tasted so horrible it *had* to be healthful, he proceeded to sell us on buying two pairs of custom boots. The clincher was the price: exactly the same as store-bought. He took incredibly detailed measurements of our feet, toes, and legs, made a tracing of them on canvas, and departed. Two months later he returned with the boots, collected his money, and asked us for names of friends who might also be interested. Turns out he comes down from his mountain home every two months, takes orders for boots from friends and friends of friends, then returns to the mountains to make boots. Two months later he's back delivering boots and taking more orders. If you can learn from a book or a bootmaker how to make boots, I heartily recommend my bootmaker's life-style.

Take a Walk

The best way to see London is on a walking tour. Same with San Antonio, San Francisco, New York, New Orleans, Paris, and any other large city you can name. (Los Angeles immediately comes to mind as an exception, but I fondly remember walking through certain sections of L.A. and enjoying it.) If you led walking tours through parts of your nearest major city, and advertised the tours in tourist publications (find them in hotels and motels and bus stations and airports), you'd be able to operate a profitable enterprise with no investment other than your own detailed knowledge of the area you intend to show, plus the cost of advertising. Such endeavors are being carried out successfully in some major cities already. So if you have an intimate relationship with your city, you can cash in on your own conducted walking tours.

Heal a Plant

The great outdoors is moving indoors as more and more people take to growing plants. Trouble is, many of these folks lack a green thumb. If you have one, you can make decent money as a plant doctor. A tiny ad in your local paper, a well-distributed circular, or a notice put in local plant stores will tell your community that you're the person to call when plants get sick. You'll probably have to learn more than you already know about plants (library), and you'll have to schedule your visits so as to allow yourself enough free time. But if you can treat sick plants and make them green and healthy again, you've got a license to practice plant medicine, and to coin money at the same time.

Chain a Tire

Money is earned by people who position themselves near the road signs that say CHAINS REQUIRED, on the way to winter ski areas. By locating their warmly clothed selves on busy highways frequented by weekend ski crowds, the chain installers make a tidy sum every snowfall. They cash in at the ski areas themselves by jumping batteries; they cash in at home by shoveling snow from cars.

Cater a Meal

If you can cook, you can cater. If you can cook and make a meal look attractive, you can cater successfully. If you can cook and make a meal look attractive and promote your business, you can cater very successfully. Again, word of mouth, small ads, and distributed/posted circulars can help your catering business. One successful catering service reaped quite a bit of free publicity because it offered not only catered parties, but also breakfast in bed for $30 (more with champagne), and candlelight dinners for two for $40. Use your imagination, then work just a few days a week as a catering service. (Be sure to check with your local board of health office for health regulations.) You can get some friends to work with you if the meal is for an especially large number of people.

Give a Massage

These days, a massage can mean a rubdown, a sexual sojourn, a medical treatment, or an insight into your psyche. The equipment necessary to give any of the above is no more than your own mind and body, plus the appropriate training (if you wish to get into the more esoteric methods of massage). There are a number of good massage books available and an awful lot of people who love to be rubbed. You can make house calls, massage in your own place, or work in a parlor. Let me know how it all turns out, huh?

Offer Yourself Part-time

Go in person to a grocery store and see if they need a part-time bag person. Try for a part-time job with a repair shop, gas station, hardware store, just about anywhere. The point here is that if you pay a personal call, you'll find part-time work much easier to come by than the full-time jobs sought by job hunters. You often can pick the days and hours. And sometimes you can get the store's merchandise at a discount. The last time I gave this advice to someone, she went down to the nearest store, which happened to be a grocery, and she got a job as a bag girl. If she was able to land a job with five minutes of preparation, I figure you might do even better with ten minutes. Incidentally, chances are you won't get the job by phone or mail. Going in person is the secret here.

Speak Something Other than English

Give language lessons if you speak any foreign language. You can give lessons in that language to English-speaking people, or you can give English lessons to non-English-speaking people, providing you understand the language they do speak. Give your lessons in groups or individually—in your home or theirs—as a part of a school or by yourself.

Tutor a Child

If you're skilled in any basic educational field, tutor kids who aren't so skilled. Often a tutor can make the difference between a child's getting accepted into college or not; the tutor can turn a failing grade into an A just by taking the time for individual instruction. The subject can be as simple as addition and division or as complex as grammar. Still, if you're good at it, sell your skills as a tutor. You don't have to be a teacher or a college graduate. But you do have to know how to communicate. In addition to tutoring kids for school, you can tutor grown-ups for citizenship tests. Early in our marriage, my wife helped us over a particularly tough financial period by doing just that.

Busk a Queue

While living in London, I well remember waiting in a long queue (line) of people waiting to see a movie. That we waited a good forty-five minutes before the queue moved one inch was no matter: There were buskers around, and my friend and I were being busked to our hearts' content. Some buskers played musical instruments. Others sang. Another did juggling tricks. And one performed feats of magic. They seemed to have divided the queue into equal parts. The appreciative members of the queue tossed out shillings and pence and even half crowns to the equally appreciative buskers. I learned then that busking is a rather commonplace English method of earning money. Whenever there is a queue, there is likely to be a busker. But not so true in the United States. So if you wish to earn extra money, and you have a talent (and guts), try busking a queue.

Be Handy

Don't just be handy in your home; be handy in other people's homes. Prepare, for your local paper and for mailboxes, a list of *all* the things you can do around a home. Then do them. The longer your list, the more likely you'll be hired and the more money you'll make. Open your mind to all the jobs around a house, and you'll find that you can do a lot more than you think. For openers, try cleaning, dusting, washing, electrical work, carpentry work, carpet cleaning, wall washing, window washing, wallpaper hanging, cooking, dishwashing, grocery shopping, furniture polishing, plastering, puttying, plumbing, painting, gardening, plant tending—I'm getting tired just thinking about it, so I'll quit here. But you get the idea.

Paint or Paper a Wall

One of the most dependable sources of income is painting (inside or out), wallpapering (inside only), or painting murals. It's a service that is always needed, and if you run a small ad, you'll get your share of work. And money.

Be Friday

Be a man Friday or a woman Friday. Offer to do all the things that a person has no time to do. Busy executives and busy housewives all have errands to run. Some can only be done by them, but many can be delegated to a Friday kind of person. It is unwise financially for many people to do their own errands and chores, but they have no one else to do them—until you. If you let it be known that you'll do personal errands for a fee, you may find yourself very much in demand (so much, that you may need a man or woman Friday to do *your* errands).

Collect a Penny

Get to know which coins are worthwhile and which are worth only their face value, then buy rolls of pennies and keep the valuable ones. You can do the same with nickels, dimes, quarters, half dollars, and stamps. Treat the coins and/or stamps not as a hobby, but as devices with which you may earn extra money.

Live in a House

Be a live-in person or couple and do odd jobs in exchange for room, board, and a small salary. You can continue your other earning endeavors, earn a bit more as a live-in, and save a bundle by having someone else pop for the food and shelter. Again, check the classifieds, and you'll find quite a few offerings.

Appear in a Movie

They make a lot of movies, and film or tape a lot of TV shows in New York, Los Angeles, and San Francisco. Features are also made in Honolulu, Chicago, Washington, Miami, and other large cities. Except for Los Angeles (which has an abundance of unemployed actors), there is a shortage of movie extras. The only cost to you is joining the right union (call a local talent agency to learn the cost), then register with an agency and hope for a call next time a movie is made near you. The pay is quite good; I know a San Francisco extra who has lived four months just off his movie-extra fees.

Remove Your Clothes

Nude modeling for art or photography classes is profitable, if chilly. Check with local colleges, art schools, or painting classes to make your availability known. These days, both males and females are needed. And your weight doesn't matter. Just your modesty.

Maintain some Greenery

A growing business is that of office plant maintenance. As plants grow in popularity, so does the need to keep said plants happy, healthy, and hearty. With just a few plants, someone in the office can tend to the watering. But with a lot of plants having different nourishment and watering requirements, and different plant diseases occurring, there is a need for a person to come around regularly and tend to the plants. Just leave your circular at every office in a particular building, and build your business, building by building. You'll make the world a prettier place, beginning with your own bank balance.

Sweep a Chimney

As people turn to alternate forms of energy, fireplaces are used increasingly, and chimneys get increasingly sooted. If you've got a good sense of balance, invest in chimney-sweeping tools and a good pair of coveralls. Then a direct-mail program to house owners or a classified ad can set you on your way.

Chart the Stars

Listen, I'm not too sure about astrology, but a heck of a lot of people are. Because astrology has something to do with gravity, and because gravity has yet to be explained, I'm not totally antiastrology. But you'd be amazed at the readership of astrology columns in the newspapers and the sale of astrology books. So it might be worth learning how to prepare an astrological chart, how to read the stars, and how other people make money with astrology (private readings, charts, and newspaper columns). The Yellow Pages where I live lists not only astrologers but also astrology schools. And California is looking into licensing astrologers the same as realtors are licensed. As I say, I'm not too sure about astrology. But I'm an Aquarius, and today's paper said I should feel free to express myself.

Read a Palm

Along with astrology as a money-earning method, I feel impelled also to list reading Tarot cards and reading palms, not to mention gazing into a crystal ball. Many people earn money plotting biorhythms and engaging in these other avenues into insight. So you may want to consider them along with phrenology (reading of bumps on heads), graphology (analyzing handwriting), and witchcraft. Every day, people earn money practicing these endeavors.

Wash a Car

While living in London, I was solicited at my front door by a young man who wished to know if I wanted my car washed each Tuesday night. I said yes. So for three years, I drove a sparkling clean car (especially on Wednesday mornings) and I never washed my own car or visited a car wash. Now, you can use your enterprising nature to build up your own car-washing or car-waxing business, offering the benefits of at-home service. Once you put in a month or so of soliciting business (door-to-door and car-to-car seem best), you'll probably gain enough business to never have to knock on a door ever again—except to collect your money. You might offer car-washing services at parking lots as well. All you need is water, a bucket, cleaning solution, and rags.

Feed an Office

Talk to the owner of a downtown restaurant and offer to provide meal-delivery service for him. Once you've got a restaurateur to partner up with you, deliver circulars to offices (with a menu on each circular) offering lunchtime meal delivery. Lots of office workers will take you up on your offer, and soon you'll probably find yourself with more work than you can handle.

Be a Casual Laborer

In California, the Department of Employment Development maintains a casual labor office. By dropping in, no notice needed, you will learn of work that needs to be done for various firms or departments. Mind you, these are not jobs; this is work. Sometimes it is just for the day. Sometimes it's for a week. But it will enable you to earn money. Check your own state to see if they, too, offer the service of a casual labor office.

Check the Union

Check your local hotel/motel/club/office workers union. They can issue you a temporary work permit that will enable you to earn money without a job at any of a number of chores. Other unions may offer the same opportunities, but I have yet to learn of them.

Deliver a Circular

By now, I imagine your Yellow Pages is dogeared from excess usage. Nonetheless, refer to it again and this time look under "Distributors." These are the people who will hire you to deliver circulars—to offices, to stores, to homes, to anywhere the circulars are destined by their mailer. The work often is day by day. And you can phone a distributor one day to see if he has work the next. Chances are he will. It's work that requires a lot of walking and a lot of carrying heavy things (a zillion circulars weigh many pounds). Still, it's work.

Vend Popcorn

Next time there's an event (concert, baseball game, basketball game, football game, any kind of game) at your local stadium, offer your services as a beer or popcorn or Coke or ice-cream salesperson. Although the regulars get first crack at the jobs, there are frequent vacancies, and you can fill them even if you're nonunion.

Sell Your Plasma

Blood is divided into two components: whole blood and plasma. You can sell your plasma at $10 per pint, and you can sell it twice a week. What they do is take your blood, then return the whole blood and keep the plasma. Your body then replaces the plasma within twenty-four hours. To sell plasma, you must never have had AIDS, hepatitis, or malaria, and you must have a valid I.D. Otherwise, there's a quick way to earn $20 per week. You can sell a pint of your whole blood, too. But there is a waiting period of a couple of months between blood withdrawals.

Manage an Apartment

Check the classified ads any Sunday. You'll find offers to manage an apartment building in return for free rent and a small salary. The work is rather demanding, but it is not full-time, and it does permit you to pursue other money-earning methods. My mother-in-law worked as an apartment-building manager for several years and she did a pretty good job. Nothing against my mother-in-law, but if *she* can do it, you certainly can.

Clean a Basement

Offer to clean people's basements, storage sheds, attics and/or closets, and lockers used for storage. Charge nothing for your services except for the junk they want you to throw away. Sell this junk to flea-market stall holders and antique dealers. Or sell it at your own flea-market stall. You'll make some money at the very worst. And at best, you'll come away with a few treasures, some too beautiful to sell, others too valuable to keep. You can offer your services on a door-to-door basis. Or you can distribute your own circulars. Or you can run a classified ad. You'd make a small fortune off the junk in our storage shed. What's more, we need you to clean it out for us because we keep getting lost amidst the old clothes and the memories.

Scavenge a Building

Check with antique dealers to determine their current needs and the latest public requests—then hie on over to some demolition companies. You can scavenge buildings about to be razed, and often come up with useful, valuable, desirable items—especially if you know what to look for. And you will.

Be a Hand

If you live near a farming or ranching community, it might be a good idea to check out the possibility of part-time employment as a farmhand or ranch hand. There is usually more work than steady jobs available, so a ranch or farm is a grand place to get into the economics of freedom. If they have nothing right now, give them your name and address and phone. They'll be grateful for your availability come harvest or roundup time. I once worked four weekends in a row rounding up horses in Colorado, then riding them up to the high country for the summertime. En route on the fourth weekend, I was thrown from my horse. I not only was thrown off the saddle, but also over a cliff and off the side of a rocky mountain. So I don't recommend that particular horse or that particular ranch. But until disaster strikes, the work can be fun.

Read a Book

Offer your services as a companion or a reader to sick, elderly, or hospitalized people. You can ascertain the needs of a local senior citizens' center, then you can make someone very happy while wiping the frown from your own bank balance. The infirm appreciate people who will spend time with them, even in silence. And you can compound the joy by reading a book aloud, engaging in conversation, running an errand, and just plain smiling.

Dive for Golf Balls

If you're a golfer, you'll quickly understand the monetary merits of plunging into the water hazards on the local golf course. If you're a truly rotten golfer, you'll recognize that this may be the key to a treasure. You can sell your retrieved golf balls to almost any pro shop for a tidy sum: perhaps as much as fifty cents a ball. When you realize that there are several *thousand* golf balls in residence amongst the murky depths of many country clubs, you can readily see that a few hours underwater might sustain you for a few months above.

Landscape a Balcony

Who says homeowners have to be the only people to hire landscape architects? Specialize in landscaping for apartment dwellers, and learn to beautify a balcony, a porch, or even a series of window boxes. Chances are, most apartment dwellers haven't a clue as to landscaping. So many of them will appreciate a true specialist in bringing the beauty of nature to good old apartment 31C. With imagination, library work, and a marketing program that includes delivering circulars to apartment buildings or mailing to apartment dwellers, you might find yourself in a thriving, growing business.

Pan for Gold

Many American gold mines closed down for all the right reasons about a century ago. Now many of them should be worked for all the right reasons: The value of gold has gone up; the value of a dollar has gone down. It doesn't require much of an investment to pan gold, nor does the required skill impose much of a tax upon your brainpower. On a recent white-water raft trip through the old gold country, I was amazed to see how many people had set up tents and sluices and were actually earning a living by mining gold. The full-scale gold rush hasn't started yet, so there are still opportunities for you. On a good weekend, you can easily earn a week's expenses in dust and nuggets.

Serve a Summons

A process server earns $30 per process served these days. All she's got to do for the $30 is hand a piece of paper to a specified person. Plus she's got to be an accredited process server. Not hard. Just ask at the nearest town, city, or county hall. Then list your name in the Yellow Pages under Process Servers, and from time to time people will call you because they've got a piece of paper for you to deliver and $30 for you to pick up.

Sell a Sign

A very practical and very successful friend once recounted how he earned quick money in a hurry (half a day). He bought a bunch of those cardboard OPEN and CLOSED door signs, walked along a few commercial streets, and offered the signs for sale to every store he passed. Because almost every store uses them, and many of their signs are yucky and soiled, and few stores keep extras on hand, and new signs look good, and new signs aren't all that expensive (my friend worked at a 300 percent markup)—he sold all his signs and could have sold more. Luckily for all of us, he is no longer in that business, so consider the opportunity unlimited. You can make even more money at this kind of work if you paint the signs yourself rather than buy them at wholesale from a dealer. You can use a stencil if you have no artistic talent, or you can use artistic talent if you have no stencil. The latter is the way to earn the most because you can customize the signs to the business by doing things like painting coffee cups for a restaurant, a shirt for a clothing store, a hammer for a hardware store, or— oh well, you get the idea.

Throw a Party

Have a plant party. Invite all the neighbors. In fact, you might even have the party at the neighbor's house. Or even at a stranger's house. The idea here is that you will offer plants for sale, offer educational material about plants for sale, offer plant equipment for sale, and fascinate everyone with a lecture on plants and plant maintenance. You can do all this yourself. Or you can act as the party branch for a local plant store. To entice neighbors into allowing you to have the party in their house, bribe them with free plants. Attendance and sales will boom if you can offer plant education by a true expert. I hope that it can be you.

Tend a Bar

Be a home bartender. Not at your own home, but at the homes of people who are throwing parties. You need to know all the mixed drinks, have a neat appearance, and a pleasant manner. Then, to develop more business, print up business cards that you can dispense as the evening wears on, but before the drinks wear off. A few ads in the classified section will get you going in the business. But be sure you do your homework and know a Bloody Tom from a Mary Collins—or is it the other way around?

Vend a Flower

Stand on a street corner during evening rush hour and sell bunches of fresh-cut flowers to homeward-bound commuters. You will do better at this if you are a female in a dress, since males will be your primary market. But even if you're a burly longshoreman in coveralls, you'll do all right if your flowers are healthy and your prices are fair. You can position yourself to serve commuters in cars, commuters about to board public transportation, or people just walking aimlessly from their place of employment on their way home. A sign that says FLOWERS $5 PER BOU-QUET will help, too. Will a sign that says FLOWERS $10 PER BOUQUET help twice as much? You'll just have to experiment to find out.

Investigate an Applicant

Many insurance and credit firms hire part-time investigators. I did the work for one semester of my college life. I earned enough that semester to pay for the entire next semester. And all I had to do was walk into dangerous neighborhoods and ask personal questions of strangers. Actually, that is exactly what I did, but somehow, it didn't seem all that bad at the time. Ah, danger isn't what it used to be in the good old days. As an investigator, you'll be requested to complete applications on people who have applied for credit or insurance. To complete each form, you need certain information. Much of this can come from the applicants themselves. But some can come only from neighbors. And you're the person hired to ask the questions. You get to choose the hours or days. All your employer cares about is the information. Good luck.

Clean an Aquarium

Ask the owner of a pet store and she'll tell you that one of her biggest headaches is dirty aquariums. You can solve this headache for her and earn money for yourself at the same time. Multiply the money you will earn from her by the number of pet stores for whom you will supply this service and you can quickly see that a river isn't the only water in which you may pan for gold.

Consult a Mover

There's money to be made in moving, even if you aren't in the moving business. Even better, you can earn money on both ends of a move. You can be a moving consultant to people about to move by helping them with securing

estimates, packing, paperwork, and being around on moving day. And/or you can be a moving consultant to people
who have just moved by helping them with unpacking,
cleaning, recommending doctors and electricians and
plumbers and veterinarians and schools and mechanics,
and being around on moving-in day. I only wish you had
been there to help my wife and me on any of our moves.
We needed you going and coming.

Tune a Car

If you know how to fix a car, fix it at someone's home and
eliminate the necessity for his having to go to a garage. By
offering tune-ups at home, you can choose your hours,
days, and the locations in which you will work. All you
need are the basic tune-up tools, good light, and time. Ads
in local papers and circulars distributed under windshield
wipers will turn up enough business for you. In this business, you will be providing a valuable service to people
who cannot do without their cars, by working on the car
while they are at home and not using it anyway. Also, you
save them the hassles of getting away from and back to a
garage.

Be a Ghost

Offer to ghostwrite a column for a local newspaper and
sign the name of a local merchant who stands to gain by
the fame a column will bring. Meaning: Write a column
on gardening signed by the owner of a garden-supply
store; write a column on interior decor by a local furni-
ture-store merchant; write a column on pets for the owner
of a pet store. Look first to your own area of expertise,
then contact merchants who sell items within that area. If
the local populace reads in the newspaper of plants and

flowers, and the column is signed by the owner of the local plant store, guess where the populace is likely to shop for new plants.

Follow Something Through

Start a follow-through service. With small classified ads, offer to follow through on items that other people start but never finish. Yard work and fence painting and car polishing and garden planting are among the billions of tasks that people tend to start but never finish. As a finisher, you ought to flourish in a sagging economy.

As I mentioned earlier, the ideas put forth here represent only the tip of the earning iceberg. The rest of it remains submerged in your own head, waiting for you to mine it.

Later in this book—in chapter 10—I'll tell you how to do the mining of ideas. Meanwhile, you can practice exercising your earning imagination by finding one companion idea for each idea set forth in this chapter. Or you can stop thinking or reading this book immediately and go to work on some of the earning endeavors already suggested.

Understand that when you try to earn money with some of these methods, you'll find that someone else already beat you to it. But in the economics of freedom, that poses little problem. For you are not limited to only one idea. You are not limited to one location. You are not limited in the multitude of opportunities that are already confronting you.

And once you have earned money along the lines outlined here, after you've paid what must be paid and spent what you felt like spending—then it will be time to amass some capital to use in opening new doors to earning. But only if you feel like it.

The old system of economics dictated that we earn money for the sake of earning money. The new system disagrees. The economics of freedom makes you the prime motivation: your pleasure, your health, your happiness. Money is only important insofar as it allows you to be more of what you are all about. Beyond that, money is certainly not useless but neither is it the idol some would have it be.

So if you are earning money by practicing some of this preaching, there may be no need to earn any more. *But—* just in case you do want some more, there are ways to earn money that can be attempted only when you have money.

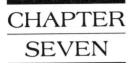

CHAPTER SEVEN

Tiny Capital Needed

One of the most winning aspects of money is that it helps you earn more money. I don't mean the way money earns dividends or interest or appreciates in value through investing. There are enough books written on these topics already. And free advice in all the newspapers.

Instead, I mean that if you have a supply of capital—say, about $3,000—you can multiply your money-earning possibilities. With $3,000, or even as little as $500, you can buy the equipment or the advertising or the manpower necessary to open lots of doors that remain locked to those with no capital. In the economics of freedom, as in the old economics, more capital equals more freedom. However, unlike the old economics, the economics of freedom does not stipulate that you need gigantic sums in order to be free. Three thousand dollars will do very nicely for virtually every money-earning method suggested in these pages. In most cases, far less than $3,000 will be required. In some cases, $5,000 will do the job a lot easier than $3,000. But in no case will you need anything like a five-figure sum in order to start the wheels rolling.

In nearly all cases, you can start out with a minimal investment. How much you go beyond this is up to you. It depends on what you already own, what you can rent, how large you wish to be at the beginning, and how quickly you wish to grow. For some endeavors, it might make sense to refinance your house, take out a second mortgage, or borrow money using your car or other valuable possessions as collateral.

As with the last chapter, for more information I direct you first to this book's appendix, then to your library, then to your bookstore, then to the federal government, then to people already earning along these lines—and finally, ultimately, as always, to your own ingenuity.

The economics of freedom requires trailblazing. Where no trails exist, you must create them.

If you feel that some of the endeavors listed in the pages following are right-sounding for your interest and aptitude, but you currently lack the capital, or enough equity for a loan, set the sum you will need as a goal. Then earn money along the lines listed in the last chapter, but be goal-oriented about it. Spend and live off the money you earn from certain endeavors—but bank the money from other efforts until you have hit your goal. Then move forward into your new opportunity.

Be careful that you do not enter a venture without enough capital. If you have $2,000, and you spend it all for inventory, that's fine. Unless you need to advertise your inventory.

The earning game becomes quite a bit deadlier when money is involved. Many people, as soon as they learn you have capital, will unconsciously tab you as ready prey, and will make energetic attempts, however cloaked in innocence to acquire that capital themselves. In some cases, the contributions of these people will more than offset their desire for your capital. They may make contributions in the form of services or time that will return your capital to you many fold. On the other hand, they may cheat you beyond belief.

The most horrifying fact of all is that their cheating generally is condoned by the U.S. business community. In fact, many businesspeople won't even recognize it as cheating, but will chalk it up to common business practice. The meaning is obvious: Cheating is a common business practice.

So guard your capital very carefully, especially from businesspeople. In chapter 2, I advised that you secure the services of a good CPA and a good banker. Ask either or both of these money managers to explain leverage, the principle by which a small sum of money garners the power of a large sum. Ask them to prepare you for all expenses, lest you find yourself undercapitalized in an unexpected situation. Because I have made grievous errors owing to my own lack of financial expertise, I now realize the enormous benefits of a smart money manager.

Understand that money has become such an integral part of human programming that it actually controls human behavior and motivates unreasonable actions in otherwise reasonable people. This seems to be true on all levels of capitalism.

The economics of freedom, by removing money as a prime motivating force, may help eliminate some financial chicanery, but until everyone understands the relationship between freedom and economics, beware—if you have any capital at all.

Recently, while working with a client of mine in the area of developing a long-range business strategy, I asked about his five-year goal for his company. His goal was to remain at approximately the same sales level as he was enjoying currently, while expending about the same effort. The effort required about three days a week of his time, and his sales were enough to sustain him and his staff comfortably. All he wanted was to maintain a Utopian status quo.

Ordinarily, any red-blooded American company wants to double or triple or quadruple its sales as part of a long-range goal. However, they rarely assess the price they will pay for that growth. This particular company did assess the price, and the people decided that giving up their free time was too high a price.

Before you embark upon your earning efforts, especially those that require capital, set your own one-year goal, five-year goal, ten-year goal, and lifetime goal. Include free time as part of that goal. Include personal enjoyment. Include caring for your health. Include family and friendship considerations. Include fulfillment of your own personality. Then include money. That's what the economics of freedom is all about—the ability to look upon money from a new perspective. Unfortunately, most companies, in establishing long-range goals, include *only* money.

While earning money *with* capital, apply the principles of earning money *without* capital. Don't limit yourself to one earning method. Don't limit yourself to the ideas espoused here. Explore whatever methods sound compatible with your nature. Then explore your own head to develop your own ideas. In fact, as you read, see if you can allow every idea that is suggested here to stimulate one more idea that comes from you.

Service a Garden

With the proper tools and knowledge, you can have your own gardening service. You can plant a garden, tend an already planted garden, landscape a yard, care for a lawn, trim shrubbery, and/or offer tree trimming. You can hire high-schoolers to do the parts that don't appeal to you, and you can spend whatever hours you wish at this endeavor. But you will need money for equipment, advertising, and bookkeeping.

Plant a Food Garden

Taking the concept of gardening forward into the economics of freedom, you can provide a unique and extremely valuable service to every home in your community: Offer to plant (and tend, if you'd like) a food garden. By careful judgment as to which fruits and vegetables will grow where and when, and by knowing exactly how to plant the seeds, you can save a bundle for your clients on their food bills while amassing a bundle for yourself and your own food bills. A six-by-ten-foot plot can produce enough vegetables for a family of four. Even an apartment can sustain a window box or porch garden. Again, you'll need equipment, advertising, and know-how. You can supply the manpower yourself—or you can farm it out to others. Also, you can charge your customers for planting only or for planting plus maintenance. Like so much else now, it's all up to you.

Sharpen a Knife

Park your van or truck, or set up your stall somewhere where you can put up a big sign informing people that you sharpen saws and knives. With good equipment you ought to do good business in virtually any high-population area.

Personalize Something

Buy an engraving machine; learn how to use it (not hard); then offer to personalize things for businesses and homes.

You can engrave names on signs, office equipment, name-plates, plaques, or diplomas. You can combine your engraving equipment with your mail-order business and offer personalized things by mail. You can also engrave title plates for framed photos or art in homes.

Play the Classified Game

Carefully read the Sunday classified section of a major metropolitan newspaper. In fact, read several consecutive issues. Keep tabs on the regular advertisers, then try offering exactly what they offer. A by-mail dating service can be run just as easily by you as by the people already doing it. You also can be a business-opportunities broker just by listing yourself as such in the classified section, then putting together prospective business buyers and sellers. You can buy goods for a low price, then sell them for a higher price—a simple economic principle as practiced in the classified sections every day. This is a little-known method of earning, but not so little known that thousands like you aren't already profiting. I run at least one classified ad somewhere every week, and as I'm learning what to say where, I'm earning more and more money at it.

Let Others Play Your Game

Buy and place an electronic video game somewhere where someone else hasn't yet beat you to it. You can go it yourself or go in with someone. The investment is a few thousand dollars, but the returns can be much higher if you've got your machine in the right place. Knowing this, keep on the lookout for potential locations.

Share a Franchise

Pool your capital, your time, and your talents in the purchase of a franchise operation in an area where you believe one can succeed. Don't buy one with the idea of running it full-time, for that is just like a job, only with more heartaches. Instead, your going-in position should be one with a head set toward sharing the work and the responsibilities. This way, you'll have your earning ambition fulfilled plus you'll have your freedom ambition fulfilled. And the same will be true for your partners.

All of you should know that the success rate for people starting their own business is less than 50 percent, while the success rate for people who purchase a franchise is more than 90 percent. The figures aren't in yet for people starting several of their own businesses. Stay tuned.

Show Your Siding

If you read the money magazines, you'll come across offers from siding companies. They'll sell you siding at a 67 percent discount with no money down if you will install the siding on your own home, then show it to prospective customers and sell it, acting as both salesperson and satisfied customer. You end up with new siding (I hope you need siding) plus a money-earning possibility. And siding is just one of many products promoted in this way.

Be a Press

A good way to be a press is to buy a press. Look in the classified section under Printer's Supplies and pick up a used printing press. Of course, you'd better know how to use it. But once you do, you can set it up in your garage, basement, or extra bedroom, and then you can publish others' booklets, courses, newsletters, house organs, or newspapers. You also can create and print your own newsletter. Example: You collect ideas that can be used by retailers, then put them into your own newsletter, print it, and mail it yourself to your own list that you developed yourself in a direct-mail program planned by you. If you're looking to become a self-contained individual, this is an excellent opportunity to start containing.

Hang around your local franchise printer for a few hours and notice how many people come in to have various writings printed: memos, newsletters, announcements, circulars, posters, invitations, stationery, and a whole lot more. You can compete with these franchised printers if you purchase or lease your own press. The field of contract printing seems to be growing, and the price of certain printing presses seems to be declining. Those two facts can be combined into a neat little (but not necessarily little) income. And look into desktop publishing.

Keep Things Clean

Make an investment in a good, professional cleaning machine, learn how to use it, advertise your services, and suddenly you can be in the cleaning business. You can specialize in carpets, upholstery, walls, auto interiors, or anything else. And you can work when you'd like.

Introduce People

Because people need people but many do not know how to go about meeting people, help them and make a business of it. An introduction service probably brings to mind a man meeting a woman. But expand your service to enable couples to meet couples, men to meet men, women to meet women, kids to meet kids, and members of special-interest groups to meet other members. For such a service, it would help to have an office, a meeting place, and planned programs. People would register by writing or phoning or paying a personal visit. The possibilities for such a service are endless. And the need is acute. The Gallup Poll informs us that 36 percent of Americans feel lonely frequently or sometimes, and 24 percent would like to have more friends. That's a lot of people who need your help. Think about it.

Breed a Guppy

Before you even consider breeding fish for fun and profit, be sure you know exactly where you'll sell them. It might be to a wholesaler. It might be to a series of pet stores. But once you've lined up customers, you can turn your basement into a guppy breeding ground. And with the proper equipment and information, you can earn a steady amount of dollars while your guppies engage in their basement orgies. Guppies are more prolific than rabbits, take up less space, and make the same amount of noise.

Be a Service Broker

Be a what? A service broker? What's a service broker? Well, in the economics of freedom, many people will be earning money by providing services: gardening, babysitting, window washing, rug cleaning, house painting, and scads of others. Many other people will need these services performed, as they always do. If the people who need the services don't see the little ads placed by the people who offer the services, how will buyer and seller get together? Good question. Glad I asked it. The answer is *you*. You will run your own consistent ads and have your

own listing in the Yellow Pages. Why, you might even
have your own radio commercials in your community. All
your ads will tell the public to call you for any needed
services. You, in turn, will have an army of contacts among
people who offer the services. Each time you give them
a customer, they give you 10 percent of their take. The
customer makes out, because he or she can be sure that
you will recommend only qualified service contractors.
The service performers make out, because they get customers without paying for advertising. And you make out
because you'll be getting a 10 percent cut from as many
service-performing people as you can line up. There.
That's what a service broker is.

Fix a Chair

If my wife can buy an old table for $15, spend about $5
on materials, devote about four hours toward refinishing
the table, and then turn down an offer of $175 for the
table because the price is too low—think of what you can
do in the furniture repairing and refurbishing business.
You won't have to buy the old clunky furniture yourself—
other people have their own. They'll just call you to fix it
up. And you'll have the right equipment and materials to
do it. Lots of courses are offered on this subject, and you
can set yourself up in a business quite handsomely for a lot
less than $3,000, including advertising.

Work in a Vacuum

With a vacuum molding machine, you can make plastic
toys, signs for just about any business, candle molds, and
other nifty things. What's more, you can do it from home
if you'd like, and you can work whenever you want. It's

worth checking into if you know anything about the business already.

Aluminize a Lens

A friend of mine lives in the desert in Southern Arizona. He has a weird-looking machine in his living room that looks a lot less weird when he tells you that he is paid $35 an hour to use it, and that he gets all the work he can handle. The machine is an aluminizer, and he tells me you can pick up a used one for around $3,000. If you can find a source of business (people who want things covered with a layer of aluminum), and you can learn how to use the machine with excellence (be an apprentice for a while), you, too, can profit from a part-time business. My Arizona buddy gets all his business from the University of Arizona, which seems to always want its telescope lenses aluminized. There are a lot of telescopes in that part of the world, so there's a lot of work for an aluminizer. But you can use the machine on more than telescope lenses. Look around your area. Ask at a nearby university. Or try some factories.

Detect Metal

I may as well tell you out front: You're not going to find any buried treasure with a good metal detector. Unless you consider the stuff that people lose in sand to be treasure. You can find coins and jewelry and transistor radios (can you imagine finding one in the sand? people do) and other assorted metal goodies on just about any public beach every Saturday and Sunday of every summer. You can use your detector to look for more exotic treasure as well, but a keen sensitivity to *where* and *when* to find the more commonplace items will lead to more certain income. And walking on the beach summer nights isn't too grim a task.

Bronze a Shoe

Seven million new American babies wear seven million pairs of baby shoes each year, and every single pair of those shoes will be outgrown. Time for you with your electroplating machine. For less than $500, you can be bronzing shoes, old pipes, baseballs, trophies, costume jewelry, leaves, insects, fruits, shells, pottery, flowers, souvenirs, tools, antiques, and just about anything else you can convince anyone to cover with bronze, silver, or gold through your informative and regular advertising programs. Without that advertising, you might have to sell. With it, you'll need only take orders. And electroplate something. To learn how, you can read books at the library or write to Warner Electric Company, 1512 West Jarvis Avenue, Chicago, Illinois 60626. You can learn porcelainizing if Warner doesn't answer your letter. That's an interesting alternative to bronzing.

Publish a Book

I did. And I didn't know thing one about publishing. I just wrote some words on a few pieces of paper, gave the paper to a person listed in the phone book under "Typographers," then brought what he did to a small printing company. I picked out a color and paper for the cover, then sold half the books to bookstores, and advertised the other half by mail order. I made money the first way, lost money the second. Then I gave the second edition of the book (10,000 copies) to a distributor who placed the books in bookstores around the country. He did that by attending trade shows, and reading up on distribution at the library. Also by hiring a few book representatives (a fancy word for salespeople). I ended up making quite a bit of money because the entire second edition sold out. I could never live off what I made with that book, but it was an early and enlightening glimpse into the possibilities of an economic system based on freedom. And without realizing it, I was a publisher. *Et tu?* If you do decide to be a publisher, you might also decide to be a distributor, and distribute your book as well as publish it. Final publishing point: If you want to play the publishing game but not the writing game, publish the writings of others. There are oodles of unpublished writers who would just love to meet up with a publisher.

Reclaim some Silver

The price of silver and gold has gone way up, and if you know where to locate useless old silver, and you have the equipment to restore it to its original pristine silver state, you can earn more money with less time spent than you ever realized. It requires information and equipment, but both are obtainable. The library tells you where. So do the income-possibilities magazines.

Install an Alarm

RRR-III-NNN-GGG!!! "Harold, it's the fire security system! I'll wake and save the kids. You put out the fire!" And Harold saves the house just because you saved the day by selling and installing a home fire security system. You can save other days and other things by selling and installing home burglar-alarm systems. Fact is, you'll probably sell and install a lot more burglar alarms than fire alarms because burglaries are rising at a more alarming rate than fires. In fact (he wrote, sadly) the crime security industry is one of the fastest-growing in America. And you'd do well financially to consider joining the industry—the security industry, not the crime industry. You can buy the equipment, learn how to install it, then sell it at a wonderfully healthy profit margin (and without too much difficulty if you do your homework about the innate value of alarm systems) almost anywhere, working almost any days, and with yourself controlling how many hours.

Recondition a Battery

If you can make friends with people at your local gas stations, repair garages, and other places where people are likely to leave their old junk batteries (junkyards, used-car lots, unkempt backyards), you can make quite a bit of money. All you need is the equipment to recondition junk batteries, the knowledge (hardly esoteric), and an outlet to whom you can sell the reconditioned batteries (try the same outlets at which you got them). Not exciting. But easy.

Remove some Snow

If you already own a tractor, snow remover, or some such mechanical equipment that can be adapted to snow removal, you can go into business every winter. Tiny ads in local papers will do the trick about getting customers. And it's a completely no-capital-needed business, except for the ads. If you don't have the equipment, then it is a tiny-capital-needed business. You'll do well if you live near a ski area or a city in which a lot of snow falls. But you'll also fare okay, with less competition for you, if you advertise in a city that gets the normal amount of snow. You won't make a lot of money. But you'll probably learn to love snow.

Maintain a Building

It can be an apartment building or an office building. It can be a factory or a public building. It can be a store or a movie theater. With the right cleaning equipment, you can offer the building maintenance services, and if you're smarter or more energetic or less greedy than the competition, you might get rich at the business. A personal mailing campaign or phoning campaign or calling-in-person campaign can net you enough business to keep you too busy for a person who wants a lot of free time.

Clean some Houses

Don't clean them yourself. You've got capital. So start a housecleaning service. First, advertise in the classified section under "Help Wanted" for housecleaners. Once you've got about three or five or ten, run little ads in the metropolitan newspaper offering housecleaning on an hourly rate. As you get orders, send your housecleaners. You must bill the person who hired the housecleaner, than pay the housecleaner yourself. Naturally, you pay less than you get, so you're making a profit every hour one of your housecleaners is working. But since you're obtaining the business for your housecleaners, you're entitled to a profit. You'll make out even better if your housecleaners are all bonded. And even better yet if you clean a house yourself every now and then.

Make and Sell Something Yourself

Make ceramic mugs yourself. Then sell them to gift stores. Make patchwork napkins with matching placemats yourself. Then sell them to department stores. Make and sell just about anything you can. You've probably got enough capital for any equipment you'd need to make things by yourself, so you can be a totally self-contained business. I know someone who designs needlepoint canvases, then sells them to needlepoint stores. I know someone who makes hanging planters, then sells them to plant stores. I know someone who makes redwood tables, then sells them to furniture stores. And you probably know people who make things themselves, then sell them themselves. What ten things can you make and sell?

Develop a Course

If you know a lot about a specific field, and you can get to a specific audience with specific media or mailings, you can create and publish and sell a course on your field. The course can be lectures, tapes, pamphlets, records, and/or books. And you can do it all by yourself. You can do the same with a newsletter on a specific topic. A man I know retired from the tire field, then published a newsletter on tires from his home. Just by dealing with the industry he knew, he was able to earn a good living without a job.

Even if you can't teach a course, you can line up experts in a particular field and create an entire course which you put not only on paper, but also on tape cassettes. It is a lot easier to learn it if you hear as well as read it. And these days, more people than ever own tape cassette players. Ideal for tape cassettes are courses dealing with music or language.

Sell Something Phony

You can (1) appeal to someone's ego, (2) make someone laugh, (3) sell something personalized, and (4) earn money without a job, if you sell and advertise phony diplomas. The diplomas can be funny doctorates, hilarious awards, rib-tickling college degrees, or sidesplitting school diplomas. They can be just about anything else you can dream up that is funny and legal. Don't sell phony diplomas that aren't patently phony or people might use them for questionable purposes. But a buddy of mine made a raft of money by selling phony diplomas with a phony degree from a phony school to real people. He had his own engraver, designed his own diploma, bought his own cheap plastic frames, and ran his own tiny ads in various magazines. Interestingly, he made more money with the idea in England than in the United States. There must be a moral there somewhere.

Rent Something Wonderful

Horses are wonderful in the country. Rowboats are wonderful on a lake or river. Motorcycles are wonderful in a tourist area. Bicycles are wonderful near a park. Canoes are wonderful on a river. Wonderful also are rafts, jeeps, skis, skates, sleds, toboggans, and other things—all wonderful in the right place. You have the capital to buy some of the equipment, store it somewhere, and put up a sign or a few ads telling the world that you have something wonderful for rent. You can work weekends only, or hire someone on a commission or slice-of-the-action basis so you need not work at all. However you do it, you can earn money easily by renting something wonderful where it is not otherwise available.

Do Something Crafty

If you can make leather goods, that's nice. If you can assemble a collection of leather goods, ceramics, paintings, sculpture, silversmithing, pottery, quilting, macramé, collages, ironwork, glassblowing, lithography, calligraphy, photography, and weaving, that's even nicer. And if you can collect these crafts as crafted by senior citizens or handicapped people or just great artists, that's best of all. Even better, you can sell from your collection on weekends only. And if you rent space in an old abandoned anything—as long as it is near where people drive on weekends, and if you offer some sort of food (pastries, sandwiches, fruits), you just may have a glorious going business. Renting an old abandoned anything near a tourist area is inexpensive and easy. Lining up craftsmen, that's inexpensive and easy, too. Running your establishment on weekends only, nothing hard about that. What are you waiting for?

Offer Something Pleasurable

Put a whole bunch of pleasurable things under one roof and see what happens. Offer massages, waterbeds for naps, electronic video game machines, bio-feedback machines, pool, Ping-Pong, stereo headphones, comfortable furniture, and anything else legal and lovely. You can let your machines support you in whatever style you would like to become accustomed to.

Send the Kids to Camp

I'm talking about your camp. Your cabins. Your counselors. Your planned activities. It's a chore that takes up seven days a week. But it takes a maximum of only eight weeks a year. Plus planning. If you know about the outdoors, have people you can trust as counselors, and can assemble some tents or cabins in an inexpensive-to-rent but lovely-to-camp-in area, you might earn enough in eight hectic weeks to last you forty-four relaxing weeks.

Send away for literature from existing camps to see what activities you might offer. My parents sent me to camp every summer. As I recall, I hated every minute of it. But the camp owners sure made out well.

Put People on TV

Buy a videotape recorder and camera, learn to use them (not much harder than a standard tape recorder), plug the recorder into a TV, and you're in business. What kind of business? Almost any kind. You can use your videotape machine to (1) add a touch of pizzazz to store promotions by putting customers on TV where they can see themselves, (2) record the growth of a child by taping him or her every six months, then selling the videotape to the parents, (3) rent to therapists as a useful new tool in psychotherapy, (4) tape small group interviews as a research tool when you know you can sell the finished tapes to companies or research firms, (5) establish a video-training vehicle for businesses that teach golf, bowling, tennis, belly dancing, archery, baton twirling, horseback riding, dancing, or just about anything else where video playback can serve as an educational tool. A videotape camera and recorder can be a fruitful source of income, and with less than $3,000 you can become a pioneer in a surefire industry. Video dating services do quite well showing tapes to people who want dates, or more.

Kill a Bug

Buy the correct exterminating equipment after you've thoroughly read up on the subject, advertise your services more proficiently than your competition, then work whenever you please. It is not that difficult a business to learn, but whatever you do, don't buy the exterminating materials until you do learn the business.

Rent a Darkroom

A whole lot of photographically inclined citizens would just love to have a darkroom where they could process their photos. But who can afford the space? Who can afford the equipment? Who can afford a snazzy enlarger? You can. And if you do, with proper advertising (not much; place an ad under "Photographic Supplies" in the classified section) you can rent your darkroom for a handsome (even gorgeous) profit. The person who first attempted this activity out in this part of the world achieved such a smashing success that several competitors burst onto the scene. But you can be the first on your block.

Take a Picture

Invest in a proper camera, professional lighting equipment, even photography lessons if you need them (and almost all photographers do), and begin taking pictures professionally: at weddings, parties, events, store promotions, bank promotions, ski areas, fishing landings, and almost anywhere else you can think of where people might want a photo as a memento. I'll bet if you photographed the homes in a neighborhood, then affixed them above a twelve-month calendar, many savvy real estate agents would be absolutely delighted to purchase your calendars so they could imprint their name and advertising theme line, then give the calendars to the homeowners as a way of striking up a relationship. Get the agents to sign on your dotted line before you take the photos. You need only one calendar to make your point—and your sale. Concept: Do it well, but inexpensively, with small but frequent advertising (in bridal shops, for example), and you ought to come out all right in the new economic system.

Invent a Better Mousetrap

It doesn't have to be a mousetrap for the world to beat a path to your door. Anything will do. Like a toothpaste or tooth powder that kids will use. Like breakfast cookies that have all the right vitamins. Like brown-bag frozen lunch sandwiches. Like inexpensive clothes. The time-honored advice to budding billionaires is to find a need and fill it. The economics of freedom would suggest that you find a need and fill it and market it yourself. And in looking for needs, try concentrating on things we all use almost every day. If you tried right now to make a list of five things that you might invent, you'd probably be amazed at your skill at dreaming up such things.

Rent a Condominium

Wouldn't it be wonderful to own a condominium on a tropical island? A lot of people do. But many of those people only use their lush accommodations a few weeks a year. The rest of the time, many of those palatial properties stay vacant. That's where you come in. Invest in a vacation to Hawaii or the Caribbean or any tropical paradise, and talk to owners of condominiums. You don't even have to go there to meet up with absentee landlords. Letters will do. Get the names and addresses of the owners from the condominium management (listed in the Yellow Pages). Offer to rent their properties while they are away. Then, armed with a goodly number of luxury vacation homes, run ads in the travel section of local papers or magazines. Each home may rent for, say, $100 per night. Each landlord might be paid, say, $60 per night. And you, for all your hard work, are profiting to the tune of, say, $40 per night. Multiply that by ten such properties, and that comes to a neat $400 per night. Even if you rent these luxury homes for only 100 nights per year, that's $40,000 for you. Minus advertising. Minus your original vacation-business trip to whatever tropical isle turns you on. There are a lot more details, but I imagine you get the gist of the idea.

Create a Medium

Make up your own advertising medium, then sell space on it to advertisers. Such advertising media might be a used double-decker London bus, benches placed strategically around town, a TV listing of the shows in your area, a local newspaper, litter cans with ads, a local classified newspaper, a kiosk, or a newsletter of local interest. Once, while employed by an advertising agency, I was approached by a man selling space on minibillboards placed in the stalls in men's rooms and ladies' rooms. The name of his company was Johnny-ads. That, I think, is carrying commercialism a bit too far. After all, we're entitled to privacy *somewhere.*

Raise some Consciousness

Develop a course such as est (Erhard Training Seminars) that puts people in touch with themselves. Advertise it, and honestly try to raise the level of consciousness of the people who attend. Such courses, if properly planned and taught, are not the shuck and jive shows that they might appear at first sight. If you honestly do have a way to make people happier and more fulfilled, build a course around it. You can prosper and contribute to humanity at the same time. It's not easy. But it is possible.

Organize a Tournament

Some people love to compete. Some people love to win. Some people love to be spectators. Make them all happy by organizing a tournament. You make money by the entrance fee. You make money by the admission charged spectators. You spend money on prizes. You spend money on rental of your tournament area. You spend money on advertising and public relations to announce your tourney. If you handle it intelligently, you make a lot more money than you spend. And you can have a rip-snorting tournament in any of many events: darts, dominoes, billiards, Frisbee, welding, cooking, baking, backgammon, Monopoly, checkers, bridge, trivia testing, tree climbing, sewing, or just about anything that has people doing it who are experts at it.

Feed a Traveler

Open a weekends-only restaurant. Put it somewhere where it can attract a lot of tourists, though that is certainly not a prerequisite for success. Offer a limited menu and do everything you can to avoid any leftovers; you won't be able to use them in your restaurant the next weekend. (You will be able to eat them at home.) With a cleverly placed sign or two, plus a tiny amount of advertising, plus excellent food, you may be able to work on weekends only. (Again, check with the board of health first.) Then you can eat out the rest of the week.

Charter a Bus

If you live within driving distance of a good ski area, consider chartering a bus, then offering ski-bus services to the skiers in your area. Chances are, they'll appreciate the freedom you provide from driving, putting on chains, jumping dead batteries, and installing ski racks. If you can fill more than one bus per weekend, you may make enough during the ski season to tide you over the rest of the year. And open your mind to running more than a ski bus. You can do the same with a beach bus, a ball-game bus, and/or a rock-concert bus. Incidentally, you won't have to drive the bus. The bus company will take care of that. All they need from you is passengers.

Teach People How to Do It

Organize a do-it-yourself course. You'll need the physical space, the materials, and the people who can teach the subject. If you talk to local craftsmen and trades people, you'll probably be able to line up a faculty that can teach people to do just about anything themselves. And these days, that can be quite a blessing. For openers, your do-it-yourself school can offer carpentry, electrical work, masonry, auto repair, plumbing, and TV repair. Those subjects alone ought to attract a lot of people who've been paying for something they'd rather do themselves.

Put Folks to Sleep

Set up a sleep department in a local department store, drugstore, furniture store, or variety store. Train the store's salespeople so that they understand the little-known subject of sleep. In your department, offer waterbeds, foam beds, sound machines, sleep books and records, snoring devices, special pillows and blankets, quilts, tranquilizing art, sleep masks and earplugs, plus whatever else you want to offer from the growing new sleep technology. Funny, after all these years, mankind is finally learning about sleep—even though humans spend 33 percent of their time asleep. The idea here is not only to deal in sleep, but to set up a department in an existing store rather than opening your own store—then to let existing salespeople do the selling. All you do is organize it and run the inventory. After all, it was your idea, wasn't it?

Keep People Warm

Invest in a good chain saw and a used truck and then go out and cut firewood. Ads in the classified section will let people know that you're in the firewood business. And with folks trying to conserve energy, burning firewood is a grand (and romantic) way to start. Your chores will be to cut the firewood, deliver it, and then (for an extra fee) to stack it. If you stack for free, you'll destroy your competition.

Serve some Coffee

Offer your delicious, fresh-brewed-coffee service to stores and offices and gas stations in your area. You provide them with a good coffeemaker and all the fixings. They provide you with a sum of money to cover your time, your equipment, and your greed, if any. No doubt, your coffee will taste far better than that from a coffee vending machine. And it will be less expensive too. Once a week, you service the machine and bring around new coffee makings. With enough customers, you might be able to pull off the one-day workweek. I know a man who runs a printing shop five days a week, a coffee service one day a week. Many weeks, he makes more from his coffee than from his printing. See—caffeine is good for *some* people.

Ride a Bike

Create a bicycle delivery service. It can start with one bike and one big basket. It might grow to ten bikes and ten big baskets, depending upon the needs of your downtown community and your rates. With ads directed to the businesses in your area, or a direct-mail campaign, you might be able to ride a bike and make a nice living doing it. Notice, I didn't say a lot of money; I said a nice living. After all, riding a bike around town isn't too horrible a way to earn money.

Set some Type

Learn how to set type, then lease a typesetting machine (or buy a used one) and let the world know that you set type for money. That will endear you to the advertising community, the printing community, the graphic arts community, the newspaper community—in fact, to just about everyone except other typesetters. Typesetting is very hard or very easy, depending upon what kind of typesetting machine you use. Some are nearly as easy as typing.

Maintain a Pool

Once a week, a man parks his pickup truck in front of my house, walks around back to the swimming pool, drops in a series of chemicals, removes weird objects with a net, and vacuums the bottom of the pool. Occasionally, he looks in at the filter and pump. For this, I am hit with a

$75 bill every month. With all due respect to The Pool Scene, the company that maintains my pool, I'd give my business to you if you'd do it for $50. Just thought I'd let you know. If you offer what is currently offered by others, but you offer it for less, you'll do all right for yourself. Just be sure you do it well. The Pool Scene sure does.

Direct a Directory

Some smart ladies in my community organized an alternative to the Yellow Pages. They call it *The People's Yellow Pages,* and it is a directory of inexpensive and timely services such as drug-abuse counseling, typesetting, abortion information, auto repair, encounter groups, swimming instruction, free food stores (true), organizers, legal help, birth control, meditation instruction, and a whole lot of other businesses that are or are not yet offered in the standard Yellow Pages. Every few years, they update their directory. And many economy-minded families keep one right where they keep the old-fashioned Yellow Pages. If your community has enough services to fit into a new directory, perhaps you can be its compiler.

Make a Postcard

Draw, paint, or photograph something that might be of particular interest to your area or in these times. Then have it printed in large quantities (not in color; not yet) on postcard stock with the appropriate words (description of front, if you want; box for stamp; name of your company; postcard; address; stock number—the latter three are optional). Next, bring it to all the merchants in your area who sell postcards and offer it to them at a truly competitive price. Some will say yes. Some will say no. By properly servicing the ones that say yes, and continuing to woo the ones that say no, you can build a thriving postcard business. You can do the same with greeting cards. A dear friend of mine, a photographer, became disenchanted with taking pictures of what other people asked him to take pictures of, and decided to take pictures of only what he wanted to take pictures of. These he turned into greeting cards, and because he couldn't think of anything to say on the inside, he left it blank. That's the whole story. And he has made a lot of money with it—an obscene amount. Don't enter the postcard or greeting-card business unless you have made a few prototypes and are assured of some orders. But if the cards you make are truly unique and excellent, you'll have repeat business for a long, long time. And most of the hard work will be behind you.

Grow a Plant

Some people earn money by buying plants from wholesalers, then selling them to retailers. Others earn money selling plants on the retail level only. Still others make their money growing plants and selling them to wholesalers. What you might consider is doing all three yourself. Using your own yard, or making a deal with farmers or ranchers to grow plants on their land, could put you in an ideal position to wholesale, retail, and/or grow your own. You'd have to do your homework as to which plants grow where and when, which plants are most in demand, and which plants can give you the greatest profit and the most freedom. But you can devote a lot of energy in the beginning, then let nature take over and provide the rest of the effort. Best of all, you'd always have the choice of growing or wholesaling or retailing and doing it as many or as few days as you choose.

Employ a Person

Compile a list of all the ideas within these pages, then try to make the most feasible ideas come alive. By attempting to offer the services to customers and the work to employees, you can operate your own employment agency. Only instead of providing jobs for people, you will be providing work. And instead of providing employees, you will be providing workers. You can operate your agency on a part-time basis and maintain your own freedom as well.

Catch a Fish

If you can arrange for a steady supply of customers, you can earn money as a commercial fisherman. Even easier, if you can arrange for a steady supply of customers, you can earn money as a seller of bait. Check the bait shops in your area, determine their needs, then try to fill their needs. If there's a lot of fishing going on, perhaps you can open your own weekend bait shop. It's worth looking into.

Be the Life of the Party

You can be the life of a lot of parties if you can hire yourself out as an entertainer for kid's parties. As an entertainer, you can be a clown, a puppeteer, a magician, a storyteller, a mime, a singer, or anything else you can dream up. Small, frequent ads will tell your community that you are available for kids' (or adult) parties. And if you have the right equipment *and* talent, you can have the time of your life while being the life of a lot of parties.

Make some Music

In San Francisco, many people earn extra money as street musicians. All it takes is talent, courage, a musical instrument, and a generous supply of passersby—well-heeled music lovers, if possible. You need not make your music on the street, however. If you as an individual or part of a group can make truly listenable or danceable music, you can provide the entertainment for parties, dances, clubs, or schools, to mention just a few places that employ part-time music makers. If you don't set your sights on becoming a famous rock star, but only plan to make a little music for a little money, you certainly ought to succeed at your ambition.

Plan a Shindig

If you give good parties, give them professionally. Professional party planners handle all the details: invitations, music, food, location, beverages, games (if any), supplies (glasses and serving plates and silver and stuff like that), decor, even the party theme, if you need one. By making arrangements with a supplier of these party items, you can offer a valuable service. And by advertising your service, you can begin to develop a list of satisfied customers. It seems to me that some of the best parties I've attended were the unplanned ones. But perhaps that's because they were planned by a true pro.

Keep a Bee

With the right information, equipment, terrain, weather, and guts, you can find yourself smack-dab in the middle of the honey business. Beekeeping can be a profitable hobby. And with research discovering more and more good things about honey, you might find yourself in at the beginning on your own land or on land you can lease from owners of large spreads.

Light up the Skies

Buy a searchlight and lease it to store owners for promotions, sales, and grand openings. The operation of a giant beam is not difficult to learn, but you do need a vehicle to haul the light from store to store. A direct-mail campaign to selected store owners, or a small advertising program, should give you enough business to get started. But this endeavor, as all others, should be thoroughly checked for competition and legality in your area. Some localities are glutted with searchlight leasing companies; others are in dire need of such a promotional device. Careful you don't get burned.

Stain some Glass

There is a man I know who takes pleasant journeys through western towns by car, and turns each sojourn into an extremely profitable business trip—though you'd never recognize the business part, so great is the pleasure. What he does is collect stained-glass windows. He gets them from razed buildings, from dealers, and from homes or other buildings whose owners are willing to sell their windows at a handsome profit. These he brings back to his affluent community and sells at a far more handsome profit. His customers are homeowners, antique dealers, contractors, designers, and architects. And he has more customers than stained-glass windows. You also can enter the stained-glass business without the long drive. That's part two of this idea. Just learn how to make stained-glass windows. It's not easy, but it's worth learning. With proper instruction and materials, you can offer your own original stained-glass windows, custom made (at ridiculously high prices) for your wealthy clientele. And you can have a load of fun working.

Reflect on a Mirror

If you have artistic ability or access to an artist, and you can make a contact with a willing mirror manufacturer, you can earn a small fortune just by visiting the most interesting places in America. Pub mirrors are becoming more and more accepted as home decor, yet few people do custom pub mirror making. You can. You can customize pub mirrors for individuals and businesses, to be sure. But you can also manufacture small pub mirrors to be sold as souvenirs in such national parks as Grand Canyon, Yosemite, Yellowstone, Mammoth Cave, the Everglades, and almost anywhere else where a souvenir store is in operation. Without taxing your imagination too much, you can come up with about ten other potential sources for souvenir pub mirrors. Again, like so many ideas—all the hard work is in the beginning: lining up the artist, the mirror company, and the customer stores. But after that part is over, you can earn quite a bit just on repeat orders.

Talk about Money

Workers now live longer and retire earlier than their ancestors. A quarter of one's lifetime may be passed in retirement. But how do the retirees manage their nest eggs? Not very well. And with very little confidence. Learn about financial management, easier than ever these days with university extension courses and new books, then counsel seniors on how they can make the most of their gold during their golden years. More than ever, older people need financial advice. You can win an appointment to begin imparting it with a well-written letter, dazzling brochure, and personal phone call. Just be sure you keep at it.

Renovate a House

An acquaintance of mine purchased a beat-up old house for $20,000. His down payment was about $3,000. Then came the hard work: plastering, building, painting, flooring, plumbing, wiring, landscaping, insulating, constructing, and all the other tough chores necessary to renovate a wreck. After two months of hard, painstaking, conscientious work, he sold the house. Price: $55,000, and worth it. With the $55,000, he bought another house, renovated it, and sold it for more than double the purchase price. If you're handy, energetic, and design-oriented enough to do the same, a lot of beat-up old houses are just waiting for you to make them beautiful and yourself rich.

Get a License

Take a real estate course, study hard, pass the test, and get a real estate license. With it, you can join up with a realty firm as a part-time salesperson, or set yourself up in your own part-time business. You have only to study how other realtors in your area operate, and then find several ways to operate more intelligently, advertise better, or provide extra services. If you do, you'll have a fine new source of income without a job. Best of all, you'll have the ability to really devote effort and earn a considerable amount of money. But you must have patience. It takes quite a bit of time to sell your first house, they tell me, unless you can figure out some shortcuts. When I first arrived in the Bay

Area, I tried to rent a house, but to no avail. Then I came upon a very clever, but new, realtor. After she failed to turn up the kind of house I wanted to rent, she started phoning people with homes for sale and asking them if they'd consider renting. Within five hours, she turned up the person from whom we eventually rented, and finally bought. Naturally, she made out well on the rental and the purchase. Cleverness counts, see?

Be a Factory

Before the Industrial Revolution, most machines were one-person machines. A person with his or her own machine could operate his or her own factory. Came the revolution, and mass production came into being. Along with it came mass unemployment and mass human insensitivity. Well, the big machines are still with us. But so are the one-person machines. And you can make many of the things giant factories make all by yourself. In fact, Sears, which used to sell one-person ice cream–making machines when it started around the turn of the century, still sells one-person ice cream–making machines. But to learn of a whole mind-boggling array of one-person machines, try the most recent issue of the *Whole Earth Catalog*. It belongs in every home where the economics of freedom may be practiced. Look through it and you'll be amazed and delighted at the wide assortment, the reasonable prices, and the lovable ability of most of the machines to be repaired by yourself with simple tools. Just leafing through the pages will stimulate many money-earning ideas. And as coincidence will have it, there will be the machinery you need to turn your ideas into reality. So try taking a few steps backward into the work consciousness of pre-Industrial Revolution days. And be a factory all by yourself.

Wash a Doggie

In Clinton, Maryland, the talk of the town is the self-service dog wash. If it sounds good to you, emulate the service. Offer sort of a self-serve car wash for canines. You'll need shampoo and flea dip, but not car wax. People who bathe their pups at home know new meanings for the word "messy." That's why dog owners shell out $15 for use of shampoos and dips, brushes, scissors, grooming shears, nail clippers, shoulder-harness blow dryers, and oh yes, plastic aprons. Spray cologne is extra. If you are thinking properly, you'll also offer a line of doggie toys, leashes, clothes, chewables, and other pup paraphernalia.

An important nuance in the economics of freedom is that of *degree of involvement*. The degree to which you become involved in one endeavor will influence the degree to which you may become involved in others.

You can dive headlong into any of the money-earning ideas suggested in this or the previous chapter, and you can maintain a high energy effort against any one single idea. At first, high energy will be necessary for just about all these ideas.

But after the idea comes alive, you will be confronted with four basic choices: (1) You can continue your efforts with one income-producing endeavor and put all your time into it; (2) you can continue your efforts with one income-producing endeavor and put just a little time into it so that you will have time available to create new and other sources of revenue; (3) you can devote as little energy and time as possible to the idea, as long as it produces some income; or (4) you can drop the idea for any number of reasons.

Of course, the proper option to choose is the one that

feels best to you. And the best choice will usually be easily spotted. Still, if you pursue number one, you may end up with a job if you're not careful. And jobs take up time and have a nasty way of disappearing. Choices number two and three seem to be most in keeping with the economic mind-set espoused in these pages. And choice number four is an option that always will be yours. Just be sure you don't exercise it too soon, since time can prove itself to be a wonderful ally if you can arrange your life to put time on your side. That's what regular advertising can do for you—bring in business with enough time. Of course, that takes enough money.

In other words, these ideas may just be springboards to far richer earning experiences and opportunities.

If you do avail yourself of them, do not lose sight of your original goals, which probably encompass more than mere money. That won't be easy. Money has a strange effect upon people: If you have a lot, you'll tend to want a lot more. Going after it may cost you the freedom that you've earned by engaging in your original endeavors.

Nonetheless, the pursuit of the dollar bill is a freedom that is allowed to anyone. And if that's what you want to do, more power to you. I hope, however, that you strike a balance between the pursuit of money and the pursuit of happiness. And I pray you never lose sight of the difference between the two.

CHAPTER
EIGHT

Earning from
Your Home

Earning from your home means earning from your house, apartment, room, tent, or cave. It does not require a lot of space.

Before you give any home-earning endeavors even an iota of thought, you've got to ask yourself whether you want to spend all your time at home. To some, that is a blessing. To others, it's a curse. Examine your head for your own attitudes.

Me, I love it. It gives me maximum freedom. It gives me access to many things that aren't found elsewhere. And it enables me to spend more time with my wife. Strangely, our marriage has improved since I've been working from home. It doesn't always work out that way for others, but it sure did for us.

Aside from cutting down on transportation and luncheon costs, working from home offers me the delicious availability of beds for napping (etc.), refrigerators for raiding, kids for communicating with, yards for wandering, books for browsing, TV for World Series-ing, cats for mystifying, dogs for loving, and a warmly heated pool for swimming. And I don't miss the commute one bit.

To be sure, there are disadvantages of working from home, too: Often they're the very same as the advantages, only looked at a different way. In addition to that, there are distracting phone calls, knocks upon the door by tenacious Jehovah's Witnesses, distractions caused by friends dropping in, kids coming by and washers-driers-dishwashers-TVs-stereos singing their disconcerting songs. Working at home takes up valuable living space (not in my case, but in many cases about to be revealed), and tempts one to do many things other than working. But the bottom-line effect for me is joy and freedom. And I consider working at home to be probably the finest fringe benefit of my economic existence.

One of the roughest aspects of working from home is that you're usually the only person around that's working. Although it is true that the other people around may have knocked themselves out with work all day, it still seems somewhat unfair to be the only worker within sight. It gives me little solace that this strengthens my character. I am not now, never have been, and never want to be a martyr.

One of the most glorious aspects of working from home is that it provides you with the ultimate freedom. You not only have the freedom to set your own hours and working conditions, but you have the virtually unlimited freedom of geographic selection. Meaning: You can make your home anywhere once you have mastered the art/science/business/discipline of working from home. If you've always wanted to live in Hawaii, now you can do it. Most of the earning ideas in this chapter can be accomplished from any home anywhere.

The development of proper discipline is probably the first obstacle you'll encounter in a working-from-home situation. I've been trying to develop this discipline for nearly five years, and I'm proud to proclaim that I'm still trying. I haven't mastered it yet. But I haven't given up, either.

On purpose, I arise at 8:15 A.M. three days a week. I do this without an alarm clock. On Thursdays through Sundays, my nonworking days, I arise later. My freedom from an alarm clock is a glorious by-product of the economics of freedom.

By 9:00, I am seated in my easy chair, sipping coffee and reading the newspaper. By 10:30, I'm ready to work. Often, I do work. Often, I find countless distractions that have no business being distractions. This is where discipline comes in. Sometimes.

I try to complete my work before sundown so that I can drive or hike somewhere to observe that sundown. During my office days, I'm not even sure I knew there was a sun. Now I acknowledge its presence with awe three mornings and three evenings per week, at least.

Because I try like mad to limit my workweek to three days, those three days are frequently long, grueling, and hectic. I try to spend two of the three days at home; Mondays I visit clients and customers and prospects and suppliers if I can fit them all into one Monday. The spillover I see on Wednesdays. And at my home whenever possible. Tuesdays are work-at-home days. Thursdays and Fridays are spent playing and wasting time, though wasting is certainly the least accurate word in this book.

Admittedly, I sometimes have to work on a Thursday or Friday. When I'm writing a book—and I've now written fourteen—I work Thursdays and Fridays. But on those days, I generally finish by around three so that I can spend the afternoon doing unworky things.

I could most likely make a lot more money, accomplish a lot more work, and build a lot more personal character if I were to do any of three things: learn once and for all to adhere to a rigorous discipline; work four or even five days a week, every week; and move my office from the dining room to a more officelike room in the house. But any of these three changes would infringe severely upon my Jayness. And that is too high a price to pay for money.

Frankly I'm a bit amazed at how few of my acquaintances earn from home. Many of them can, but prefer to work from an office or store. The reasons are many and varied: five kids, not enough space, too much strain on the marriage, too many distractions, not enough kicks at home, inaccessibility to clients, and addiction to commuting.

Working from home sounds like paradise or hell, depending upon your own situation. Don't do it unless you've given it serious thought. If you do make the decision to do it, you may have to work hours that bear a rather strong resemblance to human-being hours, since most human beings work in their stores and offices from nine to five and they may be your customers.

If you're a writer, like me, you can work any hours. But if you're an advertising consultant, like me, you've got to be near your phone at nine when office people start making phone calls. If you're into sales training, like me, you've got to meet with the salespeople during their hours, usually between nine and five. But of course if you are a public speaker, as I am, you've got to be prepared to speak whenever the group has scheduled you, and that can be from eight A.M. till ten P.M., the range I have encountered since I've added that career to my earning mixture. As you see, the more you do, the less simple are the answers to what hours you'll work. I know I should be working on Thursdays and Fridays, because that's also when the rest of the world works. But in this case, the rest of the world will just have to make a concession to my freedom.

If you do decide to earn from your home, make enough space for your efforts, then consider how you might best expend those efforts. Should you confine your home earning energies to one business, or should you carry on two at the same time? How about four? Would you believe twelve?

Many of the home-earning ventures require minor work in return for minor income. But enough minor income can cover your major living expenses. And anyhow, there are several ways to earn from home with absolutely nothing minor about the revenue that this work will be able to produce.

Similarly, while some of the earn-from-home pursuits can be started with a minimum of dollars, others require capital. Rarely more than $3,000, unless you *want* to invest more than $3,000. But some do require certain equipment or out-front investment of some sort. And all earn-from-home endeavors provide you with delightful tax advantages.

Many of the earning endeavors listed elsewhere in this book can be accomplished from home. Certainly you can teach courses in your home, set up a darkroom in your home, fix a chair in your home, and engage in several other noble money earners from home. Still, along with mail order, which absolutely can (and should, at the beginning) be started from home, the following methods of earning almost beg to be handled from home.

Clerk from Home

You can handle a plethora of clerical activities from home. For some, you'll need equipment such as a typewriter, a computer, a file cabinet (homemade will do), and a desk.

But with minimal equipment you can earn money typing, or word processing, or transcribing tapes, or filing, or billing, or collecting, or list keeping, or bookkeeping. Not a lot of space is required. And you can get customers by means of small ads in local papers or national writers' magazines, direct mail, phone calls to businesses, or personal letters. First, however, try personal contacts. A good clerical service is very helpful to a business because it can provide the solutions to problems without the concomitant problems of increased overhead.

Collect from Home

The collecting of money is one of the ugliest tasks to befall mankind. Still, someone (I suppose) has to dig graves, represent clients at divorce hearings, repossess cars and furniture, track down income-tax evaders, bust pot smokers, evict tenants, foreclose mortgages, and collect money. If you can stomach the work, you can earn money doing it—from 10 to 50 percent of whatever you collect. It's basically a business of saying powerful words by mail and telephone and sometimes in person. It is well within the law and puts horrific pressure on people. While it is true that collections can be considered a clerical chore, the function is big enough to be included as a separate money-earning pursuit. If you do it, good luck. And stay off my back.

Care from Home

Run a day-care center for kids. It is a bit shattering on the nerves, but it is fun and rewarding, too. To qualify in California, you need a license (not difficult to obtain), and a health clearance, and you must live in a safe place. Other than that, put up notes on bulletin boards, or place ads in the classified section, or list your home where other day-care centers are listed. If you truly love kids—little kids, I mean—you can perform a valuable social service and many acts of love, and make a solid contribution to your living expenses with a day-care center. How many kids you take in is up to you.

Report Weather from Home

Have you ever heard of a weather report with advertising? I haven't either, but I know of an enterprising man who makes money doing it. Apparently, he lives where you can't phone up for the official weather report. So he gets it by long distance, then gives it (by tape) when you call *his* number. Along with the weather report, he gives little commercials for local merchants. ("The wind is out of the north at twenty-five miles an hour, blowing dirt on your car, which you should wash at George's Car Wash, blowing soot on your clothes, which you should clean at Shirley's Laundromat, and blowing dust in your hair, which you should shampoo with C. J. Shampoo, available only at Glenn's Pharmacy, corner of Third and Mary. The temperature at Marvin's Delicatessen is fifty-six degrees.")

Answer from Home

Run an answering service. Local ads will net customers. Direct mail will be effective. Phone calls will do an even better job if you say something overwhelmingly motivating when you speak to your potential customers. Think about what you might say to a businessman who answers his own phone, then say it to enough people to run an answering service. Careful, though. If you have too many customers, you'll need to hire help. And that means cramping your quarters or moving your business from home.

Address from Home

An addressing and mailing service is frequently needed by businesses who want to conduct their own mailing, without the benefit of a direct-mail operation. If they can't do it themselves, they may hire you to do it for them from your home. How to let them know you exist? Address and mail something to them. While you're at it, mail your circular to direct-mail firms and anyone else in the Yellow Pages who might need you to take on a mailing task. This particular work is what might be termed no-brain work. But it does earn money.

Bookkeep from Home

I've got bookkeeping listed under clerical functions. But it is listed again because (1) it is too important a task to not be considered a full-energy function, totally apart from clerical; (2) the plummeting cost of computers now makes the equipment available to many potential bookkeepers once scared away by the high price of computing; (3) bookkeeping is one of the only words in the language with three consecutive double-letter combinations. You can learn the fundamentals of accounting from library or bookstore books. But the actual bookkeeping function varies from customer to customer. No problem. If you know the basics, you'll find the variations easy to comprehend.

Remail from Home

Advertise a remail service in newspapers far away from you, or in national publications. For some reasons (legitimate and not so legitimate) some people and companies want things they mail to come from places other than where they are. What do they do? They hire a remail service, ship a load of mail to the service, then sit back, secure in the knowledge that their mail will be remailed. What do they pay? Well, individuals with few things to be remailed pay about $1 per item. Companies with many things to be remailed pay a monthly fee, from $25 to $50 per month. Not a lot of money. Not a lot of work. In fact, you've already done the major work just by living where you live.

Research from Home

Unless you've got a computer and a modem, to research from home, you've got to leave home. But only to go to the library. Then you can come right back home with the books you checked out. The research you do can be market research, informational research, survey research (by phone, mainly, but also by mail in certain cases), and U.S. research for foreign sources. You can advertise your research capabilities in English-language newspapers. You can secure work in the States by writing to all the advertising agencies listed in the Yellow Pages, plus selected research firms as listed in the directory to the Yellow Pages. If you learn how to design a research proposal (tell a company what to research, and how to research it), then execute the proposal (see that the research is completed, then analyze it and write a report), you can charge rather huge sums. Five or six projects per year can see you through twelve contented months.

Proofread from Home

Write every newspaper, publisher, printer, and advertising agency in your area and enclose an inexpensive but unique and memorable circular telling them that you are a grand and glorious proofreader. Then be one from your home. In the mailing piece you send your customers, be *sure* you spell everything correctly.

Be Creative from Home

Any craft can be created from home. The ones most logical to pursue are those most easily sold. Making dough breadbaskets for sale on a shopping-center sidewalk is economically more creative than surpassing the Mona Lisa on canvas. Unless you have a buyer for Ms. Lisa.

Phone from Home

Establish a phoning service that provides a person with a set number of phone calls per month for a set fee. For, say, $15 monthly, a person might be entitled to wake-up calls, remind calls, and care calls in a predetermined combination. A wake-up call is one you make at an appointed time to a phone number. A remind call is a pre-agreed call at a pre-agreed time to remind someone of a pre-agreed topic. A care call is one where you phone, say, sick or elderly people regularly to check on their well-being. A local company, called Care-Ring, is performing an appreciated service and making a healthy profit with these kinds of ideas plus telephones. Small classified or display ads in local newspapers, run rather frequently, will gain the customers for you. Or rather, *should* gain the customers for you. There are no guarantees in advertising.

Repair Vinyl from Home

The money opportunity magazines have a few ads that implore you to "Earn Big Money in Vinyl Repair." I checked. And you know, it's true. If you can let enough people know that you can repair vinyl (especially people who own such things as a garage or a taxi company or a trucking firm or a big bar or restaurant), you can repair, right from your home, the vinyl that gets into a state of disrepair in cars, cabs, vans, trucks, bars, and restaurants. You can do a lot of profitable vinyl repairing if you know a theater owner, but that kind is more difficult to accomplish at home. Still, it can be done. And in every large population area, several people earn handsome incomes repairing vinyl at home. Glamorous, it's not. Realistic, it is.

Import from Home

This really ought to come under the heading of mail order. No, this really ought to come under the heading of selling. No, this really deserves a heading of its own. Importing from your home can be an enjoyable, lucrative, and uncomplicated life—if you import the right things. Through your library, your bookstore, and your business-opportunity magazines, you can learn of hundreds, even thousands, of foreign-made items. They're available. They're inexpensive. They sell at a good profit margin for you. Some even come with sales aids. What's the catch, then? The catch is knowing the good imports from the bad. The good ones sell like crazy. The bad ones drive you crazy. How to tell the good from the bad? See what is selling in your area and what appears to be on the verge of selling well. Then import items that are competitive. In price. In quality. In desirability. That's the safe way. By playing hunches as to what imported items might sell by direct mail or mail order or personal sales calls or display showings from your home—you might make or lose a fortune. The way to enter the home import business is to select one or two items and give them your all. Only expand if success demands it. Your necessary capital expenditures will be mainly for inventory and advertising. As in other forms of earning, if you've got the right product, the right ad, and the right media, you've got all you need. There is a whole world of salesworthy items. And I mean that literally. You can connect up with that world and put it to work for you, if you try.

Wholesale from Home

If you wholesale from your home, you are selling. Only instead of selling to individuals, you are selling to commercial establishments. You might wholesale imported items, or homemade items, or just about anything. You might do rack jobbing—selling a rackful of merchandise, then keeping the rack filled on a regular basis. You might give party sales—sales to a large group of invited guests. You might have your own sales force, and if you avail yourself of the mail, you can have a national network of salespeople. (Not difficult to obtain; read the opportunity magazines.) You can develop your own sales force from among groups, fellow club members, associates, friends, relatives, and strangers. In principle, you buy at one cost, sell (wholesale) at another cost, then watch someone else sell (retail) at an even higher cost. Which makes you an official middleman or middlewoman. You can even be a middlechild, I suppose.

Survey from Home

Surveying is like researching, only more specialized. Some companies hire people just to do telephone surveys, and if you'd like to know which companies, you need only write one: American Marketing Association, 60 East 42nd Street, New York, New York 10017. Ask for their list of who employs phone surveyors. Notice I have this listed in the chapter on working from home. I intentionally left it out of the chapter about businesses you can start with no capital needed. Reason: Check your phone bill the month after you start being a phone surveyor.

Customize from Home

Customize what? Van and automobile interiors, for instance. With the equipment and know-how to deal with people in just that market, you'll have your hands, your garage, and your bank account filled in no time at all. Quite a bit of information is necessary to succeed at this business. But the information is in your library, and courses are offered. And once you develop a large enough clientele in van and auto markets, you can move into other fields such as boat and camper customizing.

Sew from Home

Call the cleaners in your area; write to the clothes stores; place ads in the local classified sections. Bill yourself as a person who sews with excellence. Also, increase your profits and capabilities by offering your talent in tailoring, mending, patching, altering, embroidering, and customizing clothes. It's fun. And with a grand sewing machine, it's not all that difficult.

Upholster from Home

Upholstering is a skill that you must learn by studying from a master or a school (it's hoped that the two will be the same). But once you learn how to do it, if you advertise your ability with direct mail or inexpensive newspaper ads (display or classified), you can earn money as an upholsterer at home. It's hard to learn. But once you learn, it's easy to generate a permanent source of income.

Bake from Home

Bake an assortment of whatever you bake best: donuts, cookies, or small pastries. Bring your assortment to a selection of local grocers, bakeries, cafés, restaurants, or even flea markets. Once you've lined up enough steady customers, you can bake to your heart's content. Better still, you can bake professionally. The secret of success in this endeavor is not advertising, but quality of baked goods. One great specialty can provide sweet and steady income for a long time. And if that specialty can be mass-produced in your kitchen, such as donuts with a donut maker, you might find yourself running a first-class home bakery. Be sure to check local and state health regulations first, though.

Costume from Home

It's a whole lot more fun and creative to wear a home-made costume than a store-bought one. But it's tough to make a truly excellent costume, right? Wrong. It's a cinch for you because you're a professional costume maker. You make many because of your mailings to theater groups, and you make lots of money because of your advertising the month before Hallowe'en. Pictures of costumes you've designed are what you should show in your ads. But you knew that.

Monitor TV from Home

If you've been too busy holding down a job to notice, daytime TV is filled with soap operas. Naturally, the result is soap-opera addicts. What happens when one of these addicts misses an episode of her favorite soap opera? Chaos happens. That's why this clever lady in California thought of writing regularly published newsletter synopses of all the soap operas. You can do the same. By gluing yourself (and your VCR, or VCRs) to the afternoon serials, you can write brief summaries of the day's happenings. Then, weekly or monthly, you can publish your summaries and mail them to whoever subscribes to your soap-opera newsletter. Who will subscribe? Run some ads in the daily newspaper offering your newsletter—and the people who answer will subscribe. Run some more ads in other daily newspapers from other cities and enlarge your subscriber list. The important thing is that you or your friends must cover every episode of every soap opera. Miss just one divorce, one affair, or one clandestine relationship—and the whole newsletter may go down the tubes.

Raise Rabbits from Home

If you're interested in raising rabbits, white mice, or other laboratory animals, check with your local colleges to see if they need a source of supply. If they do not, keep checking until you can turn up people who need what you will raise. Then, with cages, space, study, and care, you can plunge into the animal-raising business. Understand in the beginning that this will be strictly for profit and not for fun. Turning a lovable white mouse over to the university psychology department may be profitable. But it is in no way fun. Ask any mouse.

Stuff Envelopes from Home

Some direct-mail companies will sell you absolutely everything you need to enter the direct-mail business, except for the labor. That you provide at home. They'll furnish you with mailing pieces, proven sales letters, envelopes, stamps, catalogs, and names of people who buy from direct mail. They even fill all the orders and mail them for you. All you do is stuff all their mailing paraphernalia into envelopes, mail the envelopes, and collect the money. If you asked whether this may become a bit boring, the answer is yes or no, depending upon what you do while you stuff envelopes. If you watch daytime soap operas, you probably won't be bored at all.

Build Furniture from Home

I know a man who retired from business. After several months of retirement, he commenced designing and building furniture in his home. At first he did it because he needed a few extra pieces of furniture. He continued because it began taking shape as a hobby. Then he sold a chair. Next a table. A few more chairs, a few more tables, and without realizing it, he was in the furniture business. Not the kind you see advertised in your daily papers, especially on Sundays. But the kind where you build what you want when you want where you want, and sell it because it's such a beautiful piece at such an honest price. He now sells all he makes, and he does it without an iota of advertising. Best of all, until his retirement he had never built a single piece of furniture. So take heart from the knowledge that if Marvin can do it, you can do it, too. Know also that Marvin converted his garage into a workshop, and invested in a buzz saw from Sears. Other than that, hardly any investment.

Read from Home

If you look in the Yellow Pages under "Clipping Bureaus," you'll find, if you live in a major city, several companies listed. These companies are hired, on a monthly fee basis, to clip all the ads and/or articles dealing with a particular subject. I once hired a clipping bureau to furnish me with all the currently published articles on sleep—as part of a project I was running for a waterbed company. I was sent a huge packet each month. Inside were articles from papers all over America, all dealing with the topic of sleep. Who, for heaven's sake, gave all those articles to the clipping service? People who read from home, that's who. And that's a way for you to earn extra money. Just call your own local clipping bureaus and offer your service. If they need a few extra readers, you've got work, and right from your own home.

Make Jewelry from Home

If you make your own jewelry, you can sell it to jewelry stores, to gift shops, or to consumers from your own crafts stall, door to door, by mail order, or by direct mail. The point is, if you can make truly professional jewelry from your home, there are many outlets where you can sell it. Pick the outlet first, then become a home jeweler.

Tie from Home

Tie fish flies from home. Sell them to local sporting goods stores or bait shops or do a mail-order try with an ad in a fishing magazine. Write to fly producers and see if they wish to avail themselves of your services. If so, start tying and earning from home.

Collect from Home

This is not a hobby book, so you know darn well that I don't mean for you to collect stamps to indulge or calm your libido. Instead, I mean for you to collect stamps as a way to earn money. With the proper study, you can turn stamp collecting into a profitable sideline. Same with coins and paintings, too. A trip to the library, just one, or to the bookstore, will set you on your way with style. A friend of mine earns his entire income as a stamp dealer.

Analyze from Home

Study up on the science (?) of graphology. Then place ads in the classified section of newspapers and psychology magazines, and in specialized magazines dealing with parapsychological phenomena, and become a professional handwriting analyst from your home. If you could analyze the type on this page, you'd know all about me. So rather than provide you with any more insights into my personality, I shall move on to still another science (?).

Chart from Home

I'm an Aquarius, and that's about all I know about myself, astrologically. But my wife, a Taurus, had a professional charting done for $25, and she knows more about herself than she wants to know. Her charting was accomplished by someone who does many charts. All for $25 per. All from home. With a lot of reading of library and bookstore books, plus attendance at a few lectures or at an astrology course, you too can chart people's horoscopes for steep fees. Is this an affront to honesty and decency? No more than religion. No more than much psychology. In fact, once we know what gravity is all about (it is rather amazing that we still cannot clearly explain gravity), we might find that astrology *is* a science. Then, perhaps, you might charge more than $25. Or you might decide to earn your income via other methods. Meanwhile, astrology, graphology, and the science of biorhythm analysis (let a computer do it for you) are ways that many people are earning many dollars from home.

Make Toys from Home

Because of the insane amount of money my wife spends each year on dollhouse furniture, I feel compelled to give her supplier some competition. Therefore, I heartily suggest that you, too, make toys or dolls or dollhouses or dollhouse furniture from home. You can sell what you make at craft fairs or direct to retail stores. And judging by what my beloved spends on things like a rolltop desk for a dollhouse den, you can make a bloody fortune. Again, without fear of becoming repetitious, let me warn you that it is very unintelligent to make a lot of toys or dollhouses until you have first lined up several customers. You need just a few prototypes to get those customers. And if your prototypes are unique and durable, you truly can earn handsomely as a provider of joy to children everywhere, including my wife.

Exchange Homes from Home

Several years ago, my wife, daughter, and I went to Chicago for a one-week vacation. A vacation in Chicago? Let me explain: There was this wedding, and this class reunion, and this business thing to look into. Anyhow, I didn't relish the thought of freeloading or paying for two hotel rooms plus rental car for a week. Still, we went to Chicago, drove round in a Buick convertible, lived in a charming three-bedroom townhouse, and it didn't cost me a penny. Why not? Because we traded homes with another family. We traded our home and car for a week, in exchange for their home and car for a week. Later, we learned that one can exchange homes with people in cities and states throughout America. You can get a list of these exchange-able homes by writing to one of the home exchange companies that most likely advertise in the travel sections of the large metropolitan newspapers near you. It's a good deal for you, good business for them, and an ideal earning opportunity for anyone. All you've got to do is compete. Advertise your own home exchange (probably in the travel section of Sunday newspapers around the country) and ask for people to list their homes with you. Everyone who lists pays a fee; everyone who wants a list pays a fee. And you make out well if you can get enough exchange-able homes on your list—to the delight of everyone except hotel and motel owners. This is now a worldwide business.

Correspond from Home

Help a lot of people feel less lonely by creating a correspondence club from your home. Advertise it in newspapers or magazines (or even experiment with classified ads), and tell people to write for your questionnaire. With it, determine their interests, then match correspondents by interest. Again, you receive a fee from each club member, and you can be doing a very good deed, indeed, if you can turn people on to each other. Understand that this is not a club for the lovelorn but, instead, is a people-pairing operation.

Water Garden from Home

From hydroponic units inside your home to white-houses outside your home, get into the fascinating (and profitable) field of water gardening: growing plants and foods and flowers and just about anything—in water that you enrich with a nutrient solution. The things you grow take root on a gravel bed, and they grow healthier, juicier, and much faster in such nutrient-enriched water, because none of their nourishment is left to chance. There are now a few good books on hydroponics. (*Beginner's Guide to Hydroponics* by James Shulto Douglas was enlightening to me.) And there are newspaper and magazine ads for large hydroponic units. Since you will be producing things that will be most likely sold by others (grocers, florists, plant shops), better check to be sure they're interested, or else you'll find yourself with a houseful of coleus and/or tomatoes.

Make Lists from Home

If you write to a few list brokers (under Mailing Lists, in your Yellow Pages), and see if they want lists of families in your town and nearby communities, and any single list broker says yes, you can earn money merely by copying names from your phone directories, and arranging them geographically. If you're willing to leave your home, you can compile even more esoteric and salable lists. Example: Cruise every street in your neighborhood, marking down the addresses of homes that need painting, gardening, roofing, screens. Then make a list of the addresses and sell them (not a difficult sale) to painting, gardening, roofing, and screen-making companies. One day of cruising can result in four lists and four list sales. Other lists you might compile would be buying guides to stores that will sell at a discount (arrange with the stores; sell the list to the public), action spots in your community or county, real estate for sale, every used car for sale; also monthly lists of new residents in your community, high school graduates list, list of homes with five-year-old cars parked in front (sell to new car dealers or car-repair firms), boat owners list, apartment dwellers list, list of owners of big houses, and more. For all of these lists there are potential buyers. And since many of the lists change from month to month, you can sell them monthly. Some may be sold to the public; some may be sold to commercial enterprises. But know that virtually all may be sold. Once you get into list making, you'll be amazed at how many lists there are to make, and how many people and companies will want the lists you compile. After all, no self-respecting capitalist wants to be listless.

Cover from Home

Put ads in local newspapers and offer to cover people's possessions with the fabric of their choice. By figuring how to cut the pattern, you can make things of color-coordinated beauty out of mundane items such as wastebaskets, vases, musical-instrument cases, little wooden boxes, lamp bases, table bases, telephones, plant hangers, bookends, big books, Bibles, atlases, bookshelves, attaché cases, pillows, and a lot more. My wife has paid many a bill for us out of her earnings along these lines. You should charge for the fabric plus your own time charges. And since you're doing custom work, your charges can be steep.

Fill from Home

Fill the blank spaces in newspapers and magazines by writing fillers: tiny articles on things like amazing happenings, recipes, household hints, embarrassing experiences, pet peeves, prayers, typographical errors, how-to-make articles, humorous anecdotes, even geographical facts. You don't need an abundance of writing talent, but you do need to know how to write grammatically correct (correctly?). By writing and mailing enough fillers, you can earn a surprisingly large amount of money. To learn of potential markets for your fillers, buy these two magazines: *The Writer,* 8 Arlington Street, Boston, Massachusetts 02116, and *The Writer's Digest,* 22 East 12th Street, Cincinnati, Ohio 45210. Leafing through them, you'll find markets for writing other than fillers, too.

Rhyme from Home

A woman in Illinois put this ad in her local newspaper: "For special occasions—birthdays, Christmas, Easter, sympathy, memorial. Your thoughts professionally expressed in a personal poem. Send $20 and details." From the ad she has received requests (and checks) for all the offerings suggested, as well as invitations, stop-smoking poems, and even gift poems. If you've always been a frustrated poet, this may be your big chance at de-frustration.

Syndicate from Home

Study a few metropolitan newspapers. Go to the library so you can check on the maximum number of newspapers with the minimum investment. Pick out the syndicated features. Sometimes they are columns. Sometimes they are comic strips. Sometimes they are puzzles. If you can figure out another feature, or do a current one better than it is being done now, write it and try to sell it (in person) to a newspaper. Then try another newspaper. Soon you might be able to market your feature by using direct mail. Naturally, it is difficult to get newspapers to commit to publishing your feature regularly. But if you get enough papers to publish, you can make a small fortune with your syndicate. Example: A newspaper may pay you $10 per week for your feature. But if you can line up fifty papers, that's $500 per week. And all it takes is one great feature idea, plus a whale of a selling job. If you've got a good

feature idea right now, give it a try. And know this: Newspapers are loath to add new features, *but* once they accept your feature, chances are it will be published for a
long, long time. Sound worth your time?

Groom from Home

Learn to groom dogs, then advertise your talent, and soon
you'll be in the dog-grooming business. And if you're good
at it, you can stay in the business as long as you'd like, with
plenty of repeat business. The way to do well is to be
proficient and to market your services well. Think of
newsworthy ways to announce the establishment of your
business; think up a nifty name—then invest in advertising it (through ads or direct mail or Yellow Pages listings
or circulars handed to dog owners or collaborating with a
pet store or a veterinarian), and before long, the dogs will
beat a path to your door. As one Connecticut dog groomer
advertises: "If your dog is unbecoming to you, he should
be coming to us."

Spin Tales from Home

Some people actually earn money by engaging in conversation via the telephone. And others phone in a bedtime
story each night. Crazy? Not so crazy if you think about
it awhile. Some folks aren't into telling a nightly bedtime
story to their kids, so they'd be thrilled if you'd take the
tale-spinning task off their shoulders. You are permitted to
make up your own stories or read from books. The conversations are those you'll have with people who just plain
want to talk to someone and listen to someone. You'll
charge a monthly fee to your customers, and guarantee
them a specified number of stories or conversations per
month. Once you place a few ads in your local paper (and

this idea is a natural for a free news story), you ought to attract enough business to keep your line busy for some time to come.

Nurse from Home

You won't make much money, but you'll make steady money if you have the room and the inclination to make part of your home a nursing home. You can care for the elderly, invalid, or recuperating. And you'll furnish them with room, board, and TLC. Check with local nursing homes in your area to determine the going rates, then consider taking in a fellow human or two, or three. And you might find that your rewards transcend the mere financial.

B-and-B from Home

Driving through England, Scotland, Wales, and Ireland, I was surprised and pleased at all the B-and-B signs I saw. It stands for "Bed and Breakfast," and that's just what it offers passing motorists. No fancy hotel rates. No expensive hotel service. Just a bed. And a breakfast. If you live on a traveled highway, and regulations permit you to offer B-and-B, it's a simple way to earn from home. And to meet some interesting people.

Deal from Home

An acquaintance of mine (I promised not to reveal his name) opens his home to weekend poker games. He doesn't play. He just deals. And provides space, and chips, and cards, and potato chips. In return for his magnanimity, he takes a teeny rake-off from each poker pot, perhaps $1 or $2 depending on circumstances. This provides the players with peace and a poker atmosphere. And it provides Mike—oops, it provides my mystery acquaintance—with money and unlimited kibitzing privileges. The same concept produces income for people who apply it to bridge, to bingo, to—would you believe—Monopoly, and, I imagine, to many other games.

Clothe from Home

If you can make a pattern for any kind of clothing, you can figure a way to mass-produce that pattern. Then, if you can keep your costs down (and you can, because you're working from your home by yourself, so you don't have the overhead of other clothing manufacturers), you can get a lot of business in a hurry. People are more value-conscious, it seems, as civilization progresses. And you'll be offering an honest value that, if you buy and create intelligently, can give you an enormous edge over your competition. Then, if you wish to give vent to your artistic talents, you can custom-design some of the garments: embroider, hand-paint, patch, knit, anything. Make a few prototypes of the clothing you might manufacture, then a few calls on local (and maybe not local, too) clothing retailers. You can build a thriving business in a short time by offering attractive clothes at low prices. It's certainly not a complex formula for success, but surprisingly few people practice it.

Board Animals from Home

You need indoor space and outdoor space, and a big heart where animals are concerned. If you have all these, you might be a perfect candidate for earning money by taking care of pets while people are on vacation. You might care for their dogs, cats, birds, fish, and whatever else—depending upon your available space. Caring means feeding, sheltering, and, it is hoped, showing affection (to a fish?). Don't take on too many animals or animals that may be incompatible with each other. Also, don't take on any animals unless you are truly capable of giving them the attention and quality care that their owners will pay you to administer.

Love from Home

As I write this, six kids are living it up in my swimming pool. They're here for the afternoon with their "parents"—who are not really their parents, but instead are paid by the county to love these kids and live with them in one big home. The "parents" display superhuman patience and understanding, because all six kids are termed emotionally disturbed. In truth, the kids seem normal, happy, and active; perhaps their original parents are the ones whose emotions are disturbed. The new "parents" act just like regular parents: providing food, clothing, shelter, advice, punishment, fun, and mostly—love. And in return, they receive a financial allotment of a given amount for each child who moves in with them. It takes a very special couple to engage in this kind of work. But perhaps you and your mate are special in that way: possess the ability to love against odds.

As you can see, earning from home can mean opening your home to others, or devoting important living space to work space, or turning your whole backyard into a money earner. You've got to consider your needs for space and privacy along with the financial considerations of all these earn-from-home endeavors. You can also try some of these earn-from-home ideas while trying other earn-away-from-home ideas.

The basic concept is that your home provides shelter and space, and you provide energy and ideas. Together, you make a glorious combination.

But whatever you do, don't stop with the ideas put forth here. These are but a sampling of ways in which people earn money from their own residences. I hope that you'll think of several more ways—depending upon the particular idiosyncracies of where you live. You can engage in different earning pursuits from home if you have a huge backyard or basement. Or a garage. Or a second floor. Or a swimming pool. Or a tennis court. Or an outbuilding. Or a penthouse. Try to take advantage of your own domicile, and adapt it to money earning. Say you have a distant and ramshackle outbuilding shack—you can rent it out to budding rock groups for practice.

You should consider your home a tool. And with proper application of tools, you can earn money. But before you start earning from home, you'd better be sure that the people with whom you share your home are in agreement with your earning plans.

If so, happy home life.

CHAPTER NINE

If You Have Wheels

If you have wheels—a car or a truck or a van or a station wagon or a bus or a jeep—you're in earning luck. If you can consider your home a tool, you ought to have no problems considering your wheels a tool.

And they are.

Even if you don't use your transportation to take advantage of some of the money-earning opportunities suggested in this chapter, you'll find your vehicle to be a boon for the many opportunities suggested in other chapters. If you're able to pay personal calls on five potential customers per day by foot, you certainly ought to double your calls by car.

If you can conduct business with three customers by foot, see if there is a way to conduct business with six customers using your wheels. Depending upon which of the opportunities you wish to explore, it is possible actually to double your income—just because you have your own transportation.

So don't limit the use of your car, bus, van, RV, jeep, motorcycle, scooter, or whatever to the money-earning endeavors coming up. Apply your wheels to all other endeavors that strike your fancy. And during the days and hours that you choose to work, try thinking of your wheels as earning tools. As such, they will provide delightful income-tax savings as well as give you the freedom to explore a whole different world of earning possibilities.

With wheels, you can conduct the identical business not only in your own hometown, but in adjoining towns, throughout your state, and/or across America. You can pay calls on an enormous geographical spread of potential customers. You can carry much of your inventory with you, and eliminate storage space at home. You can even think up earning ideas that are strictly centered around ownership of a vehicle.

To me, my car is a prime source of joy mainly because of how I use it during my free time: sightseeing the world without setting one tire onto a freeway. But I've also used it as money-earning machinery on at least fifty occasions, and for sundry uses ranging from herding horses (really) to delivering flowers and transporting wayward skiers.

And my car is a run-of-the-mill, standard U.S. car. Were it a station wagon, four-wheel-drive vehicle, or minibus, I'm sure I would have invented even more uses for it.

If you don't yet own transportation, but can earn money without a car, look into buying a car with a down payment made from your earnings, and monthly payments made from the earnings increase that a car might bring about.

If you are mechanically inclined—and I mean truly creative—you might find ways of adapting your car to perform new mechanical functions beyond mere transportation. By combining it with existing machinery, this can be accomplished. You might modify it so that it can paint stripes for parking lots. It could serve as a gardening or farming aid, properly outfitted. Certainly, your vehicle can become an advertising medium with a brilliant use of paint and/or wood, plaster, aluminum, Fiberglas.

With many of the ideas you will have, and others put forth here, you might want to consider making your vehicle your *own* advertising medium. Your only cost will be the first-time painting or construction costs. And after that, you will be in control of how many people your advertising reaches—plus which people your advertising reaches. Whither thou driveth, there thou advertiseth.

Start a Driving School

The most expensive thing you need to start a driving school is something you already have. So do what you must do to it, meet all the legal requirements, advertise in the Yellow Pages and on your car, and latch onto a goodly supply of tranquilizers or some such—because you'll need as much courage and cool as teaching ability and driving information. Park your advertisement in visible places. And try to think up a name for your company that will put you as the first listing in the Yellow Pages. Aardvark would accomplish that in most communities. But perhaps "Aardvark Driving School" doesn't quite conjure up the confidence that "American School of Driving" does. I'll just have to leave the details up to you.

Start a Flower-Subscription Service

Many offices (and some homes) always have fresh flowers around. From whom do they get the flowers? From the florist. But isn't delivery often a hassle? Certainly. That's where your flower-subscription services come in, and thrive. Delivering flowers on a regular basis is what you're all about. You secure subscribers by personal solicitation, direct mail, or handing out circulars. Then you go to your local flower market—the place where the florists go. You buy your set amount of flowers. And you deliver them regularly: to offices each Monday morning, to homes each Friday morning. You can conduct this business totally on your own. Or you can offer yourself as an adjunct to any local florist.

Start a Shopping Service

Many elderly, invalid, wheel-less, or otherwise nonambulatory people would appreciate it very much if you'd take care of all their shopping for them. Mainly food shopping, but other kinds of shopping as well. These people would even pay you a set fee for every shopping excursion you embark upon. All they have to do is find out about you. They will if you advertise in the classified section, or any other newspaper section that elderly, invalid, wheel-less people might read. I'd probably experiment with the TV section. You would vary your charges by the difficulty and extent of the shopping list. And you'd be performing valuable chores for a small but grateful segment of your community.

Start a Delivery Service

You can deliver just about anything people pay you to deliver, as long as you've got the room in your vehicle. You can place ads in the Yellow Pages to accomplish that. Or you can specialize in certain kinds of deliveries and use the daily papers to advertise that you deliver, let's say, desserts. You might become the master of three different desserts, make them fantastically well, and advertise them so that the reader's mouth waters upon exposure to your ads. By making a limited number of items in bulk, you decrease your costs as well as gain a reputation for expertise in those limited items. You might specialize in delivery of diet meals only—tailored to a perfect balance of deliciousness and conscience. You might offer your delivery services to an existing anything—from a hardware store to a drugstore to a Chinese restaurant. Or you could run your very own service. Or . . .

Start a Mobile Restaurant

Understand at the outset that I don't mean for people to eat in your vehicle. What I mean is that people will eat what you bring them in your vehicle. And what you bring them can be what you make or what a restaurant makes. It's easier if the restaurant takes care of all the meals. It's more lucrative if you take care of all the meals. You can run your business whatever days you wish, as long as you keep regular days. (And again, check with the local and state boards of health for restrictions.) If you offer a wide selection of meals, I hope you deliver out our way.

Start a Touring Service

Good luck. If you live in a beautiful or historic locality, if you live near tourist attractions, or if you can dream up any other reason to inaugurate a service to compete with Gray Line—get a chauffeur's license, obtain a limousine permit, and comply with whatever other twists and turns the red tape takes. Then create a one-hour tour, a three-hour tour, a full-day tour, and a clever marketing program. You might want to curry the favors of major hotel doormen or bell captains. You might want to advertise in tourist publications. You probably would benefit if you could distribute circulars at airports and bus depots. You should attempt to show, with your car or van or even limousine (if you can trade in for a used one), all the things the big sightseeing buses can't show, along with the best of the things they do show. You should attempt to show a few "discoveries" on your tour. If you create an interesting enough ride, you can charge pretty stiff prices. And if you play your cards properly, you won't even have to be the driver after a bit. You'll attract enough business to hire drivers, and maybe even to buy another car or two.

Start a Mobile Maintenance Service

Drive from home to home to home to home and provide weekly home maintenance services, or even monthly services. Guarantee to spend a specified number of hours per week (or month) in return for a specified fee. Keep your tools in your vehicle, and make yourself available to do odd jobs. Offer this service to businesses as well as residences. Warning: If you keep your tools in your car, keep them in the trunk, or hidden beneath a nondescript cloth. The sight of them might cause your car to be broken into. If you're good at providing maintenance services, and if your scope of services is broad enough, word-of-mouth advertising will work wonders for you.

Start to Service Vending Machines

The servicing of vending machines (collecting the money, repairing, cleaning, filling) is a very common method of earning without a job. But it is barely worth considering unless you have wheels. With wheels, it is very worth considering, considering how many machines you can service. You can easily determine the needs for your servicing services if you call some of the phone numbers you find on vending machines in your

area. Or you can call up all the companies listed under
Vending Machines in your Yellow Pages. Much as I try
to restrain myself, I cannot help but caution you not to
take any wooden nickels.

Start a Hauling Service

I don't mean a moving service; later on I do, however.
Here, I mean for you to invest $35 or so in a trailer hitch,
then offer your services to tow and haul things for other
people. I'm thinking in terms of towing a horse trailer (it
cost me $75 to accomplish that one year, and I would
gladly have given the business to you), a boat, another car,
or someone's rental trailer. Many people with small, imported cars find that their car is too small to haul their
large boat. If your car is more powerful than theirs, your
car can earn extra money for you this way. Tiny ads in the
classified section will help you. So will announcements
posted on the bulletin boards of boating clubs.

Start a Traveling Department Store

You might want to skip this section if you're the owner of
a small car. But if you own a large, large car, or a station
wagon, or especially a truck of almost any sort, you can
own and operate your own department store. You can
carry any items you wish. And if you service small, back-
woodsy towns—the kinds without their own Macy's or
Neiman-Marcus—you might become a mobile Macy's of
your very own. Naturally, you will select the items to sell
on the basis of the needs of the towns you will service. If
the merchandise you offer is unusual enough, your marketplace just might be anywhere in the entire United
States.

Start an Antiques Dealership

A friend of mine earns a healthy living driving through towns in the West and buying up old advertising signs. Then she resells them to dealers at incredibly inflated prices. Join her. You don't have to limit yourself to advertising signs. Begin to collect almost any kind of antiques: bottles, doorknobs, lamps, telephones, photos, postcards, old grocery items, glassware, silverware, doors, you name it. The larger your vehicle, the greater your earning potential. Be sure you know for certain that you can sell what you buy. But even if the dealers don't buy your offerings, you can probably make out well with a stall of your own at a flea market. To drive lazily through the old towns of America, knowing that you are earning all the while, is a rather paradisiacal pursuit of cash. Before you leave, check with antiques dealers, who will gladly tell you exactly what to look for—providing you promise to offer them first rights of refusal.

Start a Security Patrol

You may be at a loss to capitalize on this idea if your car happens to be a sports car. Still, if you paint an official emblem on the doors, and call yourself a security patrol, you can get paid for providing that service. You've got to contact the powers that be in certain communities, subdivisions, housing projects, or minisuburbs. Then, with their blessings (and money), you can patrol their neighborhoods as a crime preventer. If you see any evidence of criminal behavior, you'll have to notify the police, unless you are licensed to carry firearms. And be careful that your car doesn't look policelike. That is against the law. The idea is to stay on this side of the law, and to see to it that others do the same. You can also offer your patrolling service to

factories, golf courses, almost anywhere crimes are com-
mitted. And unfortunately, that's almost everywhere.

Start a Plant-Running Service

It is one big hassle for the owners of plant stores to go
down to the plant market several times a week. That's
why they'll probably pay you to accomplish the plant runs
for them. If you can line up enough plant-store owners,
you can line up a pretty decent income. It will help if you
know everything there is to know about plants. But the
store owners will gladly furnish the knowledge if you furnish the transportation. You need not limit your service to
plants, either. Whoever has to pick up supplies on a regular basis will most likely be very happy to learn that you
will do their picking up for them.

Start a Subscription Service

Just as store owners often buy certain items on a regular
basis, people do too. Some of the unfaltering purchases
they will make on a steady basis will include toothpaste,
toilet paper, soap, milk, eggs, breakfast food, detergent,
and a whole lot more. You can save them the time and
trouble of buying these items; you can probably even save
them money—if you enable them to subscribe to these
products, and you deliver them regularly. If you can buy
in bulk, you can save money for your subscribers. And if
you have enough subscribers, you can keep some of these
savings for yourself as well as passing some on. If you
cannot buy in bulk, you'll have to charge a flat fee for your
subscription service. The idea is new, but you'll be surprised at how warmly accepted it will be by many who
resent their regular shopping trips and would be glad to
pay you to cut down on their shopping time.

Start a Moving Service

You've probably already figured that you can offer this service if you own a truck. But even if you own a mere automobile, you can rent a trailer and operate your own moving company. It takes muscles. It takes friends. And it takes a listing in the Yellow Pages plus a regular classified ad to put you in charge of a small moving company that can return more than a small return. The friends I refer to are the people who will help you carry all the heavy stuff, and naturally they'll expect to be paid. Still, you can make out surprisingly well, especially if you can offer your moving services in areas where you have little competition.

Start a Service Service

Become a traveling barber, a traveling stylist. Try your hand at being a traveling masseur, a traveling mechanic, a bike repairman, a TV technician, a house painter, an autobody fixer. Almost any service that can be provided can be provided more conveniently by one who makes house calls. So make them. Naturally, the more services you provide, the more business you'll attract. But it is more important to provide superior service than a wide range of service. By making house calls, you'll already be in possession of a competitive edge. So be sure your talent is equal to your convenience.

Start a Transport Service

Advertise that you will transport anyone anywhere as long as it is on a regular basis, and see what happens. You may hear from commuters. You may hear from mothers of schoolchildren. You may hear from almost anyone who has to get from here to there, and is willing to pay you to take him. It's worth looking into, and it may be an easy way to earn easy money. Don't forget, whenever you transport people for money, you've got to have a chauffeur's license. Not difficult to obtain. Incidentally, I recently saw an ad by someone who wanted to hire a service such as this to transport elderly people around on a regular basis. The customers are out there. All they've got to do is find out about you.

Start a Commuters' Commuting Service

Here's a timely and increasingly needed application of the last earning idea. During these unhalcyon days of an energy or financial crisis, this endeavor seems to be a natural: Pick up commuters at their homes, take them to their commuting train/bus, and then pick up and deliver them back home again at day's end. A small direct-mail program aimed at a small geographical zone should net you enough customers (you can mail or deliver the literature on your service). And if you have a five-passenger car, you can handle about twenty customers per day, at five runs per morning and evening. Your service will be appreciated by the commuters, who will no longer have to make their mad dashes to the bus/train stop; your service will be warmly accepted by the wives of the commuters, who had to perform this service before you had your bright idea. You can charge a monthly fee for your pickup and delivery service, and for just a few hours of driving time per month you can pick up some handsome change.

Start an Errand Runnery

Bill yourself as Errands Unlimited or something similar, and let it be known that you are available to run almost all kinds of errands with your willing attitude and your wheels. You will find yourself asked to do such things as grocery shopping, across-town delivering, kid picking up, odds-and-ends hauling, and just about any other errand you or your clientele can think up. It may keep you hopping, and it probably won't be a bit boring.

Start a Water Delivery Service

Whatever you do, *don't* look at a drop of your drinking water under a high-powered microscope. But if you do happen to give a drop a microscopic examination, take a picture of what the microscope sees, then show that picture to all your neighbors. If you live in a community not famed for the purity of its drinking water, you soon ought to have a line of customers a mile long. And they'll all want to sign up for your pure-water delivery service. Once a week, you'll drop off several gallons of crystal-clear, delicious drinking water in big bottles, several bottles to each subscriber's doorstep. With ads in local newspapers, you ought to gain more business than your car can handle. So you can buy a truck with your earnings. As pollution increases, so will your business. Lucky for you. Unlucky for us.

Start a Bottle-and-Can Recovering Service

As you slowly drive your car along major highways and through popular picnicking areas, you will be able to recover a wealth of returnable or collectable bottles, plus all too many seamless aluminum cans—the kind they pay you money for. You can sell your bottles to grocers or antique dealers, depending upon the age of the bottle. And you can sell the cans to reclaiming centers. Best of all, you can help keep America a whole lot cleaner, and make money while you're at it. This business is a whole lot easier to operate if you have a partner who drives while you collect bottles and cans, or vice versa.

Start a Magazine Distributorship

Actually, you will be operating more of a delivery service than a distributorship. But after a while, you might want to expand your delivery service into your own distributorship. Meanwhile, contact some magazine distributorships in your locality and offer to deliver magazines for them. With steadily rising postal costs, they may be all too happy to hire your service. Many magazines have had to cease publication because of postal prices. Many others are on the brink of collapse. As the magazines go under, so do many distributorships. But you, with your trusty van, can save the publishing world—or at least one magazine, or at best, one distributor. Your delivery fees, even if steep, will probably be far less steep than the current cost to mail just one magazine. Incidentally, you should charge on a per-magazine-delivered basis. And no fair peeking at centerfolds.

Start a Snowplowing Service

I well remember my winters in Chicago. The memory is not fond. It is even less fond when I remember my snowed-in driveway. Where were you then with your snowplowing service? By attaching a device to your car, you could have cleared my driveway, and you probably could have been paid for clearing everyone's driveway on my street. In snowy climes, it seems that whole communities would be more than glad to sign up for your snowplowing service.

Start a Winter Sightseeing Service

I realize that this chapter deals with wheels. I also realize that snowmobiles have no wheels. Once over those hurdles, I wish to suggest the earning possibilities of your own snowmobile: sightseeing, winter delivery, even a minitaxi. If you own your own snowmobile already, I'm sure you can think up even more commercial uses for it. But please follow these two suggestions: Don't snowmobile past my house during the morning, because the noise will awaken me, and be sure you wear gloves, earmuffs, a hat, and a nice, warm muffler.

Start a Location-Scouting Service

Certain people earn money by driving around and finding locations where TV shows or movies may be shot. These people advertise their service to the film community, and the film community is delighted to avail itself of the service. Recently, I was very impressed with a location finder whom I know. She was given the assignment to find a restaurant in the San Francisco area that could serve as a typical restaurant in Madrid. The next day, she came up with a suburban country-club restaurant that looked more Spanish than any restaurant I saw during my Iberian sojourns. She earned her scouting fee, and you can too—if films are made in your community.

Start an Expedition

This one is for four-wheel-drive vehicles only. Sorry, Cadillac owners. If you live in an area with back roads that can only be handled by four-wheel-drive vehicles, and those roads lead to interesting places, you can run one- and two-day exploring and camping and archaeological and fishing and hunting and photographic and bird-watching expeditions. Such services are thriving in many desert areas as well as mountain locales. The more ambitious your expedition, the more equipment you'll be expected to provide. And at the very minimum, you'd better be able to provide camping and survival gear, plus an intimate knowledge of your terrain. If you think you might enjoy running such expeditions, consider moving to an area where you might run them. It's a free country. And if you practice the economics of freedom, it is even freer.

I hope the ideas here will give birth to a lot more ideas of your own. Certainly, they are not an exhaustive list of all the possibilities of money earning with a vehicle. Instead, they are meant to stimulate the creation of an exhaustive list.

Some things that you might consider, however, may be beyond the capabilities of your current vehicle. In that case, no problem.

Trade your car in for a tow truck. Or a delivery van. Or a taxi. Or a jeep. Or even a motorcycle with a sidecar, if you can find ways to earn money with that. Trade in your new car for an old bus, if bus owning appears to be your key to financial independence.

Remember that as you are not locked into your current job, you also are not locked into your current vehicle. You have the freedom to take on work instead of a job. You have the freedom to drive a van instead of a car. Tailor your possessions to fit your earning needs. And tailor your earning endeavors to your essence.

That is what freedom is all about.

CHAPTER TEN

What to Do Now

The first thing to do now is to decide exactly what it is that you should do now.

The hardest, and most important, thing is to *do* it. It is the doing that will separate the freedom achievers from the freedom spectators. And freedom is not a spectator sport.

When you complete this chapter, you should be armed with a list. That list should serve as your map to freedom. But before you create your list, there are certain attributes you have that can help you immensely.

Some of these attributes are well-known to you, and you have most likely been using them for most of your life. But others of these attributes, although yours, may never have been put to work for you. Now is the time to pull out all the stops and use absolutely everything you've got going for you. And you've got a lot.

Use Your Energy

You'll need all the energy you can muster to devote to what begins right now. By understanding your attributes and realizing how to combine them with your possibilities, you will gain a whole new perception of your future.

With this perception, you will see how very much in control of your life you really are, and then you will be able to determine the exact steps you must now take.

The first step to freedom begins with comprehending that it is yours. Yes it is. *It is.* No matter how else it appears, your life offers total freedom.

Deciding how you will achieve that freedom is taking another step toward it. Then actually doing the things you've decided to do is the step that begins to break the shackles called "job."

Following through. Doing what you've decided. That takes a load of energy. If you want freedom enough, you'll need that energy. Just know right up front that it will be tapped to its greatest depths.

Use Your Luck

You can become lucky if you know how. And here's how: Realize that *luck is a combination of preparation and opportunity.* And you're in control of both.

Preparation for the economics of freedom would include amassing as much information and equipment as you will need for all the sources of income you choose to develop. Opportunity would consist of the selling and marketing of your goods or services.

By conscientious preparation, and vigorous development of opportunity, you will begin to become lucky. Business will be attracted to you in time, and you will soon handle it with professional aplomb. Is it really luck that will contribute to this success?

Of course it is.

Use Your Unconscious

Your mind is the source of conscious and unconscious power. Although we sometimes exercise nearly 100 percent of our conscious power, we rarely do it more than five or six minutes an hour. The rest of the time, our mental states are semiconscious: relaxing to our brains, yet productive to a degree.

Our unconscious power, however, is relatively unexploited. It is the source of all our involuntary functions, plus the nesting place for our memories and knowledge. But as a source of ideas, this huge reservoir of information and power is rarely tapped.

It can be put to productive use. And anyone can do it. It's a three-step process:

1. If you need the solution to a problem or the creation of an idea, write down all your thoughts on the matter. Try direct conscious thinking at first—thinking of the problem at hand or the obvious ideas that spring forward. Then try indirect conscious thinking—lateral thinking. Write down thoughts that are connected to the problem, but not the problem itself. Read what you've written.

2. Muster up all your conscious power and try to solve your problem. Try to create your idea. Really give it a go. Spend a bit of time concentrating on solutions. Think up as many as you can. Then . . .

3. Turn it all over to your unconscious. How? By forgetting it. Forget all about it, and move on to a different activity. Anything. Put your mind anywhere but on the problem at hand. In time—not a very long time—the solu-

tion will pop into your head! Beautifully clear, and who
did it? You did it—with your unconscious mind. There's
no telling when the solution will be revealed by your
unconscious to your conscious mind. It can happen while
you're eating, while you're working on a different problem, just before you drop off to sleep, first thing as you
wake up, and even at the most unlikely moment of all.

If you haven't yet let your unconscious mind do a lot
of your problem solving for you, there's a delicious sur-
prise in store for you. Our unconscious minds are probably
capable of a great deal more than we can comprehend.

Use Your Awareness

The main thing you must be aware of is the needs of
society. Turn your awareness on to this. Tune in to what
is happening and will happen next. Naturally, you must be
aware of your own abilities. Naturally, you must have an
awareness of your own needs before you even determine
what it takes to make you free.

Are you aware of your own power yet? Do you know
how much you can achieve as an individual? My wife
designed a new kind of picture frame, and, because she
didn't know enough to be nervous, took it right to the
proper buyer at a fifty-store chain. The result was a
$3,000 order.

Background: My wife had never designed anything
before, had never dealt with the business community
before, had never sold anything to anyone before. My wife
had never done anything vaguely like designing and selling a product for a major retailer.

Her own power floored her. She couldn't think of a
reason why she could design a picture frame. But she
couldn't think of a reason why not. She couldn't think of

a reason why the buyer of a huge chain would want to see her. But she couldn't think of a reason why not. She rarely had been aware of her power as an individual. But when she needed it, she didn't doubt her power.

For all of us, it can be the same. Even though we may never have been aware of our power as individuals, nonetheless, that power is there. And it will remain ours to use *until we doubt it.*

By the time my wife received her order, she was aware enough of her capability as an individual to establish and accomplish production of her frames in a thoroughly professional manner because she had become aware of her power. You will accomplish much, much more than you can imagine if you can only become aware of the power you possess right now.

When I was working in the world of big business at an advertising agency, and I was still drenched behind the ears, I was amazed at the lack of talent in the upper echelons. Out of about a hundred executives in the company, I found that I respected only about four. When I asked a fellow beginner for his impressions, he too felt admiration for only about three or four of the hundred. The longer I continued on in the world of business, the more I realized that four first-class people out of a hundred is a pretty good average. So regardless of your inexperience, be confident and aware of your own abilities: You're as good as the competition and your customers, maybe even better.

In addition to awareness of your own power and abilities, you need an awareness of the future. If you're aware of it, you can prepare for it. So use your awareness to determine if you can set up a business that you can own.

If you own it, you might be able to sell it, you might be able to will it to your family, and/or you might be able to retire on the income it provides after you've ceased being active. Some businesses, even though owned, are worthless if the principal is the person who does all the work. So, if you need to provide for future income, try to establish a source of income that will continue to produce income after you're too old, lazy, or unmotivated.

Some businesses do this automatically; others never can achieve it. You must be aware of your own needs plus the capacity of your business to provide income after you cannot.

But as I mentioned before, the key awareness is an awareness of the needs of your community, your planet, and your time in history. If you can fill the right need at the right time, you ought to make a fortune. And only a keen awareness of what's needed can tell you what and when.

Naturally, you must always use your awareness of all the legal implications of any earning activity (and there are usually plenty), and your awareness of the competitive situation.

There are some times when lawyers must be sought out. It is their job to protect you from legal monstrosities, many of which do not truly exist except in the minds of the legal profession. They can help immensely in many situations. But they also can muddy issues to the point that the issues are no longer understandable. I hope you will always be aware of both the joys and pains that can be inflicted by lawyers in the economics of freedom.

Use Your Intelligence

Intelligence is the ability to adapt to new situations. The better able you are to recognize a new situation as being new, the more you will be able to adapt to it. And if you can adapt properly, you will be using your intelligence in a most productive manner. By practicing the economics of freedom, you will have one terrific advantage over practitioners of traditional economics. That advantage is flexibility.

You will be able to move fast, to adapt quickly, to make the right changes at the right time. Larger firms tend to be more ponderous, more tradition-bound, more governed by committees and procedures, more inflexible. This gives you a grand opportunity to use your intelligence and adapt to changing needs.

And if you never grow too large yourself, you will always have the advantage of a usable intelligence.

Use Your Imagination

Be amazing.

The more amazing you are, the more you will succeed. When you do not have the brute force of a gigantic advertising budget, you must turn to the brute force of your own imagination to communicate your abilities or goods.

And the way to exercise that force is to be as amazing as you can.

There are some people who are paid large sums just to be amazing. Jim Moran is one. He sold refrigerators to Eskimos to prove how amazing he is. A young couple who had just opened a boutique lacked the money to advertise it properly. So they got married in their boutique. The ceremony was covered on TV and in the newspaper. All free publicity—and just because they were amazing. It does not require talent or brains to be amazing, merely courage. But brainpower should not be overlooked. Someone great once said that if you wish to call attention to yourself, you can accomplish that by coming downstairs with your socks in your mouth. By which he meant that merely calling attention to yourself isn't enough. You've got to be amazing about your particular offering. If you manufacture fake-fur bikinis, and you can get a shapely lady to model one of your creations on a winter day downtown, that's being amazing with a point to the amazement. And that's what your imagination should do for you: Create amazement with a point to it.

Imagination. Everyone has it. Let your unconscious mind show you just how fruitful your imagination is. Then have the guts to bring the fruits of your imagination alive.

Use Your Capital

You are blocked from many income-earning ventures by the lack of capital. So carefully consider your sources of capital if you wish to expand the freedom you currently have. The first places to look should be right in your own bank account, then your stocks, bonds, mutual funds, and similar investments. Consider a second mortgage. Consider refinancing your house or condo.

Check the cash value of your insurance. Consider the financial potential of a garage sale. Think about selling some possession or putting one up as collateral for a loan. Any of these can provide enough capital to open hundreds of different opportunities. Check government sources, too.

Determining what, if anything, you will sell in order to gain earning capital will help you get a good fix on your sense of values. If you can't come up with any source, talk to your money manager. If you can't afford or don't understand the need for a professional money manager, engage in a pursuit requiring no capital until you can afford the services of a financial consultant of proven ability.

There are a great many lines of work that require capital for you to enter them. But you can enter many of them even if you have no capital.

You do it by leasing or renting the equipment you

ordinarily would have to buy or own. With intelligent planning, you should be able to generate enough income to cover the cost of a monthly rental payment. If you don't own a car and can't afford a used car, perhaps you can afford a leased car—if the use of the car will cover the cost of the lease.

Take a walk through a nearby rental store and check its equipment and price list. That ought to be worth five earning ideas right there.

And the more earning ideas you have, the more freedom you have. If you can use your capital to activate these earning ideas, you will be controlling a process that can result in the most liberation you have ever experienced.

Use Your Knowledge

Use the knowledge you have gained from this book. It has been compiled specifically to give you greater access to freedom.

There are many other books that can add much to the knowledge imparted here (and a number are listed in the appendix). Some deal with survival while out of work. Some talk of the personal power that you have within you. Others deal with the nitty-gritty of the work you might undertake: restoring antiques, getting the most out of your computer, free-lancing, collecting advertising antiques, buying at garage sales, holding garage sales, running a flea market, selling, running a day-care center, growing plants, importing, wholesaling, gardening, and literally hundreds of other pertinent topics.

I've mentioned many times the wonders of your library or local bookstore. Browsing around their business sections and their general/practical sections, you'll find a treasury of earning ideas along with the details on activating them.

Invest a couple of dollars to buy magazines such as *Entrepreneur* (2392 Morse Avenue, Irvine, California 92713), *Income Opportunities* (380 Lexington Avenue, New York, New York 10017), *Opportunity Magazine* (6 North Michigan Avenue, Chicago, Illinois 60611), and *Money-Making Opportunities* (Success Publishing Company, Inc., 13263 Ventura Boulevard, Studio City, California 91604). Watch out for the offers made by advertisers in those magazines. Some are perfectly legitimate and others are spurious. But the editorial matter is generally very helpful.

Talk to people who are already in full control of their lives, people who have demonstrated *both* a good business instinct and a passion for freedom. The two often do not go hand in hand.

The earning knowledge that you now have and that will gradually increase is knowledge that should do more than merely enlighten you. It must also be put to use.

Use Your Feelings

What you feel is a good indication of who you are. And what you do should ideally be an extension of who you are. So let your feelings guide you at first.

Be sure when you make a written list of your earning endeavors that you go with those where you feel most comfortable. Later, you will use your intellect to home in on these endeavors. And by putting your feelings in writing, you will be providing nourishment for your intellect.

If you feel positivity about only one earning activity, be sure you realistically appraise the potential income it will provide. Many businesses fail because they provide for only one source of income.

The economics of freedom is formulated around the concept that, in most cases, only multiple income sources will assure economic survival along with freedom from an impersonal economic system.

If you select multiple sources of income for yourself, be sure the sources are compatible with one another. Your intellect will pave the path to freedom dictated by your feelings. For instance, it is highly impractical to attempt to engage in home plant maintenance along with conducting walking tours. But it makes a lot of sense to combine an endeavor such as proofreading with running an answering service. Both can be accomplished at the same place, and probably at the same time.

Given a choice of engaging in an earning pursuit that feels right but does not offer high financial returns or one that feels awkward but offers rich financial benefits, your long-term happiness will be best served by the lower-paying labor of love. By engaging in the lucrative pursuit, you may consider yourself free, while in actuality you are a slave to the dollar. Be honest with yourself. That's what feelings force you to do. And I hope you are in touch with your real feelings. Some people never truly are.

Use Your Freedom

Use your freedom to set your own goals. That is a freedom you already possess.

Set a work goal—the kind of work that will make you feel fulfilled. Set a money goal—a monthly income that can provide a comfortable life by your own definition of comfort. Set a time goal—just how much time you wish to devote to earning.

Consider limiting your work hours. And limit them any way you wish. Perhaps you wish to work three days a week, as I do. Possibly you can limit your work to three weeks a month. It may feel best for you to work mornings only. Or evenings only. Think about a work schedule that keeps you active eight months a year. Or maybe one that will enable you to work diligently for two years out of three. The choices are yours. And the nine-to-five, five-days-a-week job mentality need not apply to you. Freedom of working hours is reserved for those without jobs.

Use your freedom to set a five-year goal. Ask and answer: What do you wish to be doing five years from today? Be as specific and detailed as possible with your answer. Set a ten-year goal as well. By setting long-range goals, you will more clearly see the way to achieve them. And you now can have the freedom to set any goals you wish.

Use your freedom to pursue the leisure activities that now can become part of your life. See if there is a way to turn a leisure activity into an earning activity.

Many people are doing just that. Where there were about 13 million small businesses in 1980, now there are 20 million. The most recent survey, by American Express Small Business Services and the National Federation of Independent Businesses report that 77 percent of nearly 3,000 businesses surveyed were still in business after three years. This is a definite reversal of the statistics from the 1970s.

More important, 90 percent of the business owners said that if they could do it over, they would go into business for themselves all over again. And most important, 78 percent of the business owners said their primary motivation for starting their own firms was to have more control over their lives. Sounds reasonable to me.

Most of the money-earning examples in this book come from my own tiny part of the world: Northern California. Although I did not intentionally attempt to limit my suggestions geographically, I discovered many of them by merely looking around.

So look around your section of the world and find a whole new world of earning possibilities. Keep yourself in

contact with the rest of the world as well. Do it by expos-
ing yourself to all the media: newspapers, TV, radio,
magazines, movies.

If you are to be sensitive to the needs of society, you
will have to be armed with as much knowledge as possible. This book provides some. A great deal more will
continue to come your way through our increasingly so-
phisticated media.

Once you have set your goals—in writing—finalize a
list of the income pursuits that will enable you to achieve
these goals. Then put into writing the exact steps you must
now take to begin to earn income with these pursuits.

The moment you take the first step, the moment you
make a conscious decision to take all the steps—that is the
moment that you take over control of your life. And once
you have that control, you will have freedom.

Appendix:

Publications That Can Help You

Books

Accounting for Non-Accountants. John Myer, Hawthorn Books, New York, New York.

America's Centenarians. Social Security Administration, Washington, D.C. 20064. (14 volumes.)

Books in Print (subject guide). R. R. Bowker. New York, New York. (Another standard reference that is available in libraries and bookstores.)

Direct Mail and Mail Order Handbook. Darnell, 4660 Ravenswood Avenue, Chicago, Illinois 60640.

Dome Simplified Bookkeeping Record #612. Dome Building, Providence, Rhode Island 02903.

Effective Selling Through Psychology. Buzzota/Lefton/Sherberg. Wiley-Interscience, New York, New York.

Entrepreneurship: Playing to Win. Gordon Baty. Reston Publishing, Reston, Virginia.

Everyday Law Made Simple. Jack Last. Doubleday, New York, New York.

555 Ways to Earn Extra Money. Jay Conrad Levinson. Henry Holt, New York, New York.

221

The Foxfire Book (and *Foxfire 2, 3,* and *4*). Anchor Press/Double-day, Garden City, New York.

Guerrilla Marketing. Jay Conrad Levinson. Houghton Mifflin, Boston, Massachusetts.

Guerrilla Marketing Attack. Jay Conrad Levinson. Houghton Mifflin, Boston, Massachusetts.

Guerrilla Marketing Weapons. Jay Conrad Levinson. Plume, New York, New York.

Handbook of Everyday Law. Martin Ross. Harper & Row, New York, New York.

The Home Office Guide. Leon Henry, Jr. Home Office Press, 17 Scarsdale Road, Scarsdale, New York 10503.

How I Raised Myself from Failure to Success in Selling. Frank Bettger. Prentice-Hall, Englewood Cliffs, New Jersey.

How to Make Money with Your Home Computer. Glenn Gilchrist. Information Resources Unlimited, West Islip, New York.

How to Sell Well. James Bender. McGraw-Hill, New York, New York.

How You Too Can Make at Least $1 Million (But Probably Much More) in the Mail-Order Business. Gerardo Joffe. Advance Books, Box 7584, San Francisco, California 94120.

Illusions. Richard Bach. Delacorte Press/Eleanor Friede, New York, New York.

The Magazine Index. Information Design, Ltd. (This is an index machine that helps you locate magazine articles; you'll find it in most libraries.)

The Modern Accountant's Handbook. Edwards/Black. Dow Jones-Irwin, New York, New York.

The Ninety-Minute Hour. Jay Conrad Levinson. Dutton, New York, New York.

The Right Work. John Caple. Dodd Mead, New York, New York.

101 Businesses You Can Start and Run with Less Than $1,000. H. S. Kahm. Parker Publishing, West Nyack, New York.

On Your Own. Kathy Matthews. Vintage Books, New York, New York.

Quit Your Job! Jay Conrad Levinson. Dodd Mead, New York, New York.

Readers' Guide to Periodical Literature. H. W. Wilson, Bronx, New York. (This is a standard reference book and is available in most libraries.)

The Rogue of Publisher's Row. Edward Uhlan. Exposition Press, New York, New York.

Scratching Your Entrepreneurial Itch. Peter Channing. Hawthorn Books, New York, New York.

Self-Reliance (essays). Ralph Waldo Emerson. Carlton Press, 84 Fifth Avenue, New York, New York 10011.

Small is Beautiful. E. F. Schumacher. Harper & Row, New York, New York.

Small-Time Operator. Bernard Kamaroff. Bell Springs, Laytonville, California 95454.

A Treasury of Business Opportunities. David Seltz. Rockville Center, New York.

Ulrich's International Periodicals Directory. R. R. Bowker, New York, New York.

What Color Is Your Parachute? Richard Nelson Bolles. Ten-Speed Press, Berkeley, California.

Whole Earth Epilog. Random House, New York, New York.

Manuals from the Entrepreneurs Institute, 2392 Morse Avenue, Irvine, California 92713. (List of manuals detailing how to start numerous businesses; also has valuable data on SBA loans, ideas for businesses, legalities.)

Periodicals

Adweek Books (a free catalog). Tel: 800-3-Adweek.

Annual Register of Grant Support. Marquis Academic Media, 200 East Ohio Street, Chicago, Illinois 60611.

Entrepreneur. Entrepreneurs Institute, 2392 Morse Avenue, Irvine, California 92713.

The Futurist. World Future Society, P.O. Box 30369, Bethesda Branch, Washington, D.C. 20014.

Income Opportunities. Davis Publications, 380 Lexington Avenue, New York, New York 10017.

Money-Making Opportunities. Success Publishing Company, 13263 Ventura Boulevard, Studio City, California 91804.

Opportunity Magazine. 6 North Michigan Avenue, Chicago, Illinois
  60611.
Specialty Salesman and Business Opportunities. Communication
  Channels, 307 North Michigan Avenue, Chicago, Illinois 60601.
*Standard Rate & Data Consumer Magazine and Farm Publication
  Rates and Data.* Skokie, Illinois.
Venture. 35 West 45th Street, New York, New York 10036.
The Writer. 8 Arlington Street, Boston, Massachusetts 02116.
The Writer's Digest. 22 East 12th Street, Cincinnati, Ohio 45210.

Seminars

Marketing Professional Services, New York University School of
  Continuing Education, 380 Lexington Avenue, New York, New
  York 10017. (This course is offered nationally. Call 800-223-7480
  for a free brochure.)

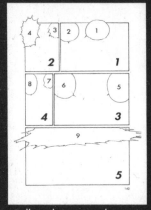

Hey! You're Reading in the Wrong Direction!

This is the **end** of this graphic novel!

To properly enjoy this VIZ graphic novel, please turn it around and begin reading from **right to left.** Unlike English, Japanese is read right to left, so Japanese comics are read in reverse order from the way English comics are typically read.

Follow the action this way

This book has been printed in the original Japanese format in order to preserve the orientation of the original artwork. Have fun with it!

W9-ASH-51

POKÉMON™

☀ SUN & MOON ☽

Story
Hidenori Kusaka

Art
Satoshi Yamamoto

Sun dreams of money. Moon dreams of scientific discoveries. When their paths cross with Team Skull, both their plans go awry...

PICK UP YOUR COPY AT YOUR LOCAL BOOK STORE.

©2018 The Pokémon Company International. ©1995-2017 Nintendo / Creatures Inc. / GAME FREAK inc. TM, ®, and character names are trademarks of Nintendo.
POCKET MONSTERS SPECIAL SUN • MOON © 2017 Hidenori KUSAKA, Satoshi YAMAMOTO/SHOGAKUKAN

POCKET COMICS
Legendary Pokémon

STORY & ART BY **SANTA HARUKAZE**

FOUR-PANEL GAGS, POKÉMON TRIVIA, AND FUN PUZZLES BASED ON THE CHARACTERS FROM THE BEST-SELLING POKÉMON BLACK AND WHITE VIDEO GAMES!

Available now!

To the forest! To the sea! To Legendary Island!

Join our Pokémon pals on their quest through Unova— while testing your knowledge and laughing all the way!

Ask for it at your local comic book shop or bookstore!

ISBN: 978-1-4215-8128-6

www.PerfectSquare.com

www.viz.com

©2015 Pokémon.
©1995-2015 Nintendo/Creatures Inc./GAME FREAK inc.
TM, ®, and character names are trademarks of Nintendo.
BAKUSHO 4KOMA DENSETSU NO POKEMON O SAGASE!! © 2013 Santa HARUKAZE /SHOGAKUKAN

Splatoon
The Turf Wars have started in Inkopolis, and the team that inks the most ground will be crowned the winner!
Based on the hit Nintendo video games!
1
Splatoon
STORY AND ART BY
Sankichi Hinodeya
STORY AND ART BY
Sankichi Hinodeya
TM & © 2018 Nintendo.
SPLATOON © 2016 Sankichi HINODEYA/SHOGAKUKAN
RATED A ALL AGES
VIZ
viz.com

From the pages of
Nintendo Power™ magazine,
a full-color graphic novel
inspired by the classic
Super Mario Bros.™
video games!

SUPER MARIO ADVENTURES™

Story by **KENTARO TAKEKUMA**   Art by **CHARLIE NOZAWA**

The peril-plagued Princess Toadstool is kidnapped by the diabolical deadbeat Bowser but super plumbers Mario and Luigi hatch a plan with their new friend Yoshi to rescue her. Are the Super Mario Bros.' plans a pipe dream? Can they stop the Koopa King before he forces the Princess to be his bride?!

TM & © 2019 Nintendo.
SUPER MARIO ADVENTURES MARIO NO DAIBOKEN © 1993 Charlie NOZAWA, Kentaro TAKEKUMA/SHOGAKUKAN

THE LEGEND OF ZELDA™

A LINK TO THE PAST

STORY AND ART BY SHOTARO ISHINOMORI

LONG OUT-OF-PRINT, THIS STUNNING, FULL-COLOR GRAPHIC NOVEL IS NOW AVAILABLE ONCE AGAIN!

An adaptation of the beloved, internationally-bestselling video game originally released for Nintendo's Super Entertainment System! This comic book version by Shotaro Ishinomori (*Cyborg 009*, *Kamen Rider*) was first serialized in the legendary *Nintendo Power*™ magazine.

TM & © 2017 Nintendo.
THE LEGEND OF ZELDA: A LINK TO THE PAST.
© 1933 ISHIMORI PRO/SHOGAKUKAN

viz media
viz.com

THE LEGEND OF ZELDA

LEGENDARY EDITION

STORY AND ART BY

AKIRA HIMEKAWA

The Legendary Editions of *The Legend of Zelda*™ contain
two volumes of the beloved manga series, presented in a
deluxe format featuring new covers and color art pieces.

® & © 2016 Nintendo. ZELDA NO DENSETSU TOKI NO OCARINA (KANZENBAN) © 2016 Akira HIMEKAWA/SHOGAKUKAN.
® & © 2015 Nintendo. ZELDA NO DENSETSU FUSHIGI NO KINOMI DAICHI NO SHO, JIKU NO SHO (KANZENBAN), ZELDA NO DENSETSU MAJORA NO KAMEN (KAMIGAMI NO TRI-FORCE (KANZENBAN),
LDA NO DENSETSU FUSHIGI NO BOSHI (MIGEN NO SUNADOKEI (KANZENBAN), ZELDA NO DENSETSU ITSU NO TSURUGI PLUS (KANZENBAN) © 2016 Akira HIMEKAWA/SHOGAKUKAN.

THE LEGEND OF ZELDA

・TWILIGHT PRINCESS・

Volume 7—VIZ Media Edition

STORY AND ART BY
Akira Himekawa

DRAWING STAFF mati. / Akiko Mori / Sakiho Tsutsui

TRANSLATION **John Werry**
ENGLISH ADAPTATION **Stan!**
TOUCH-UP ART & LETTERING **Evan Waldinger**
DESIGNER **Shawn Carrico**
EDITOR **Mike Montesa**

THE LEGEND OF ZELDA: TWILIGHT PRINCESS
TM & © 2020 Nintendo. All Rights Reserved.

ZELDA NO DENSETSU TWILIGHT PRINCESS Vol. 7
by Akira HIMEKAWA
© 2016 Akira HIMEKAWA
All rights reserved.
Original Japanese edition published by SHOGAKUKAN.
English translation rights in the United States of America,
Canada, the United Kingdom, Ireland, Australia and
New Zealand arranged with SHOGAKUKAN.

Original design by Kazutada YOKOYAMA

The stories, characters and incidents mentioned
in this publication are entirely fictional.

No portion of this book may be reproduced or transmitted in any form or
by any means without written permission from the copyright holders.

Printed in the U.S.A.

Published by VIZ Media, LLC
P.O. Box 77010
San Francisco, CA 94107

10 9 8 7 6 5 4 3 2
First printing, August 2020
Second printing, September 2022

PARENTAL ADVISORY
THE LEGEND OF ZELDA is rated
T for Teen and is recommended
for ages 13 and up. This volume
contains fantasy violence.

AUTHOR'S NOTE

This year (2019) marks the milestone of 20 years since *Ocarina of Time* began serialization in Japan. Thank you for your support for so long! Our first long series, *Twilight Princess*, is finally moving toward its climax. Now that Link has overcome various tests he faces the final battle with new determination. What kind of drama will Link, Princess Zelda the Princess of Hyrule, Ganondorf the King of Darkness, and Twilight Princess Midna show us? What kind of hero will Link become? Please keep reading!

Akira Himekawa is the collaboration of two women, A. Honda and S. Nagano. Together they have created ten manga adventures featuring Link and the popular video game world of *The Legend of Zelda*™. Their most recent work, *The Legend of Zelda*™: *Twilight Princess*, is serialized digitally on Shogakukan's MangaONE app in Japan.

VERY
WELL.

I WANT TO FIGHT LIKE YOU.

WHO IS GANON-DORF?

WHY DO I HAVE TO DEFEAT HIM?

WATCHING THE FIGHT JUST NOW, I UNDERSTOOD.

WHO AM I WHO WEARS THESE GREEN CLOTHES?

THERE IS A VOICE IN MY HEART.

I HAVE NO UNNECESSARY FEAR OF FACING MY ENEMY.

I CAN ACCEPT THE WAY I AM NOW...

....WITHOUT RESER-VATION.

...AND GANONDORF WAS EXECUTED BEFORE HE COULD DO ANYTHING...

THEN PRINCESS ZELDA TURNED BACK TIME SEVEN YEARS...

I DEFEATED GANON-DORF.

I FOUGHT BACK AND FORTH ACROSS TIME, SO SOME CALLED ME THE HERO OF TIME.

THIS TEMPLE WAS ONCE THE PLACE WHERE I TRAVELED THROUGH TIME.

HISTORY CHANGED AND THE FIGHT BETWEEN GANONDORF AND ME NEVER OCCURRED.

...SO NO CATASTROPHE BEFELL HYRULE.

ASIDE FROM PRINCESS ZELDA AND ME, NO ONE KNOWS THIS.

WHAT YOU SAW EARLIER WERE EVENTS IN A FLOW OF TIME THAT BRANCHED AWAY AND BROKE OFF.

NO...

...TO BE PRECISE, THREE PEOPLE, INCLUDING GANONDORF, ARE AWARE OF IT.

...!

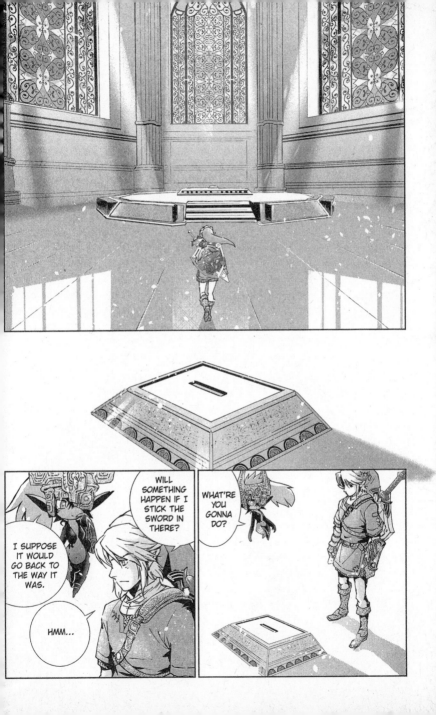

KREEEAK

KREAK

LOOKING
FROM
BEHIND...

NOTHING.

THAT'S
ODD.

#40. THE TEMPLE WHERE TIME SLEEPS

NO!
I WILL END THAT HERE.
WITHOUT FAIL!
SMASH
HE IS COMING.
I FEEL EACH MOMENT.
SO I WILL GIVE HIM A FINE RECEPTION!
I AM GOING TO BREAK THE CHAIN HERE!

THE TWILIGHT REALM WAS A FAR BETTER PLACE FOR CULTIVATING THAT DARK AMBITION.
BUT THERE WAS ONE PROBLEM.
I DID NOT KNOW A WAY TO RETURN TO THE LIGHT. AND THEN...
...I FOUND SOMEONE WHO HARBORED A SIMILAR AMBITION ...
... BESTOWED JUST A LITTLE POWER...
...AND HAD HIM INSTIGATE A REBELLION AT THE PALACE AND OPEN A PATH FOR RETURNING TO THE WORLD OF LIGHT.
IT'S ALL GOING...
...ACCORDING TO PLAN.

...AND THE ROYAL FAMILY OF HYRULE GAVE BIRTH TO ANOTHER GIRL AND NAMED HER ZELDA.

THERE WAS PEACE THEN, AND THE PEOPLE'S MEMORY FADED...

...AND BEFORE YOU COULD DO ANYTHING, HAD YOU EXECUTED TO PREVENT CALAMITY IN ADVANCE.

...AND THEN, WHEN YOU, WHO KNEW NOTHING, CAME FOR AN AUDIENCE WITH THE KING, I HAD YOU CAPTURED...

HEH...

THEY ORDERED THEIR VASSALS NEVER TO ALLOW *ME* TO BE INVOLVED WITH THE TWILIGHT REALM.

THEY SAID THEY HAD BURIED THE DEMON THIEF GANONDORF IN THE TWILIGHT REALM, NEVER TO RETURN.

MY PARENTS—THE KING AND HIS WIFE—DID NOT TEACH *ME* THIS DARK HISTORY. THEY HID IT FROM ME.

YES...

...WHEN I...

WHEN DID YOU REMEMBER ALL THAT?

OR SHOULD I SAY, WHEN DID YOU COME BACK TO LIFE?

I'M HAPPY FROM THE BOTTOM OF MY HEART THAT WE COULD MEET.

TRULY.

HOW DID YOU COME BACK TO LIFE?

YOU WERE EXECUTED ALMOST 100 YEARS AGO.

THEY EXECUTED ME IN THE DESERT AND SENT ME TO THE TWILIGHT REALM ON THE ORDERS OF THAT ERA'S KING OF HYRULE.

AND THE ONE WHO ADVISED THE KING TO EXECUTE ME WAS...

YES, WELL... I HAVE A LONG-STANDING GRUDGE AGAINST THE ROYAL FAMILY OF HYRULE.

THE *CHAIN* THAT BINDS US WITH THIS DETESTABLE TRIANGULAR MARK...

...APPARENTLY NEVER BREAKS...

...NO MATTER HOW MANY TIMES I DIE OR EVEN IF I FALL INTO HELL ITSELF.

OR SHOULD I CALL IT A CURSED AND CORRUPTED CONNECTION?

NO.

DON'T LOOK SO DISPLEASED. DON'T WE GO WAY BACK?

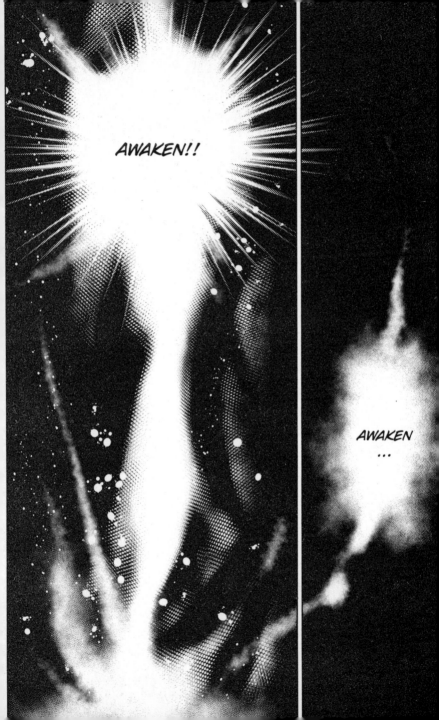

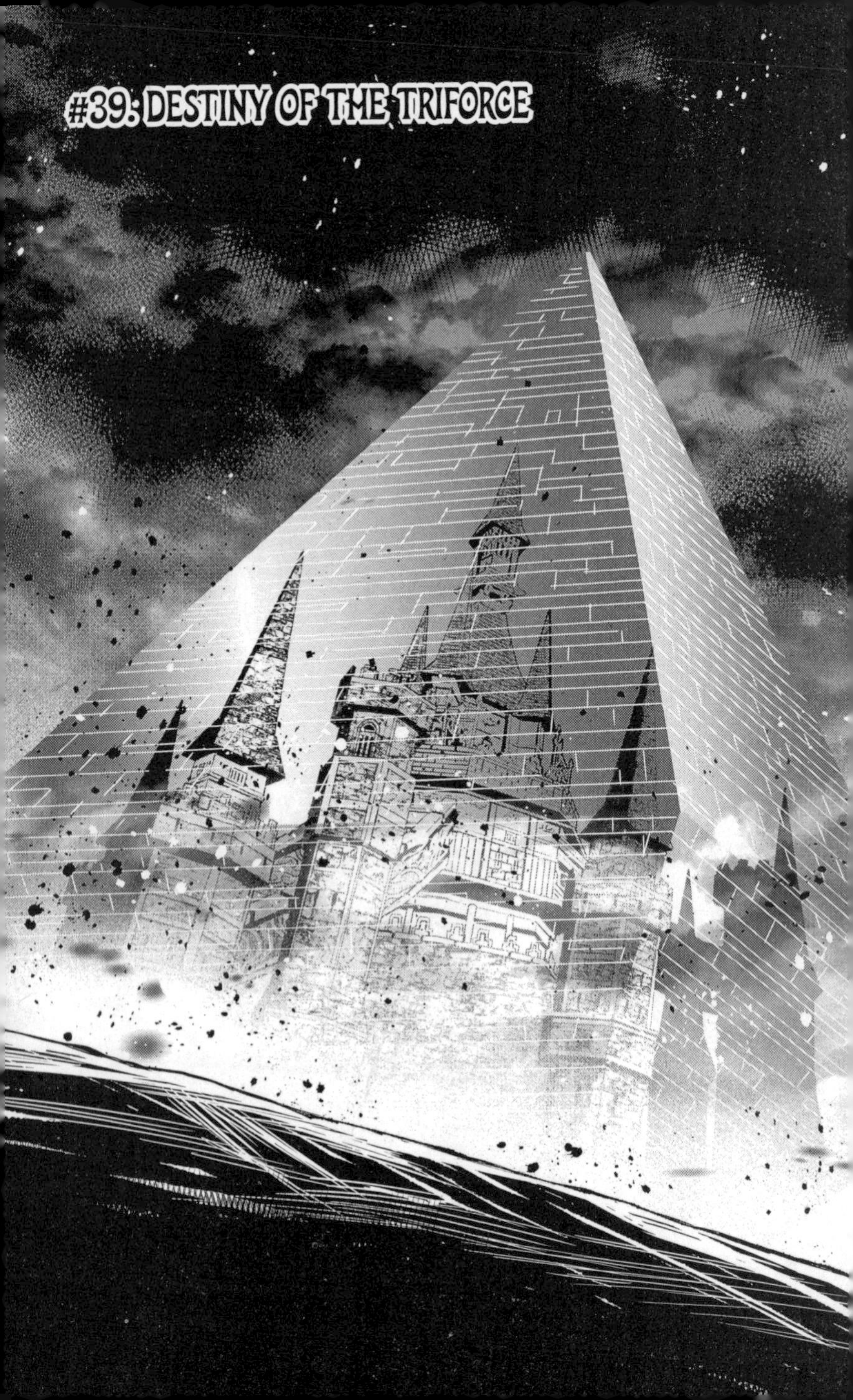
#39: DESTINY OF THE TRIFORCE

WHP

HARUMEHI LEAF!

FLUTTER

FLUTTER

FLUTTER

FLUTTER

HOW LONG HAS IT BEEN...

...SINCE I FELT THE WIND?

#38. SETTING OUT ON A JOURNEY AGAIN

FWSH

KREAK

W-WAIT!

...A LITTLE LONGER!

DON'T GO! LET'S TALK...

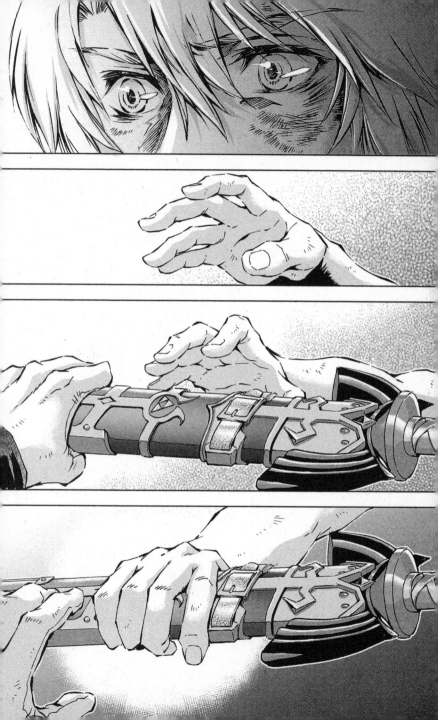

MONSTERS ATTACKED ME AND I BECAME A WOLF...
...I HAD TO GO THERE AND COLLECT THIS AND FIGHT THAT, AND WITH ALL THESE SPARKS FALLING ON ME, I NEVER THOUGHT ABOUT WHAT I WANTED.
TEST ... AFTER TEST ...
...AFTER TEST!
I'VE HAD ENOUGH! SET ME FREE!
WHY?
WHY?!

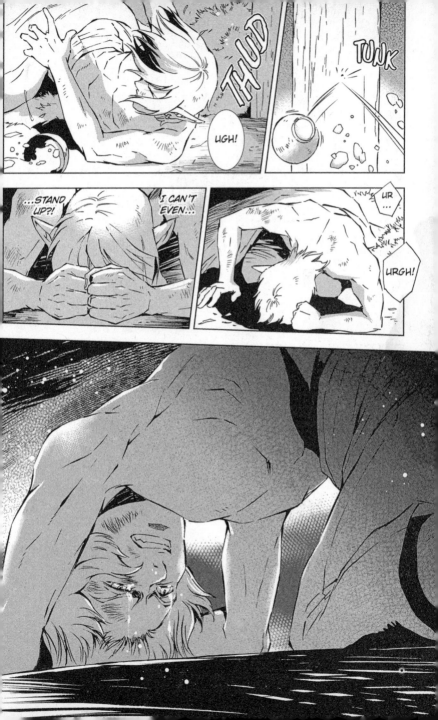

#37. INVITATION TO REBIRTH

THE LEGEND OF ZELDA

ZELDA

7

·TWILIGHT PRINCESS·

STORY AND ART BY

Akira Himekawa

TM & © 2020 Nintendo.

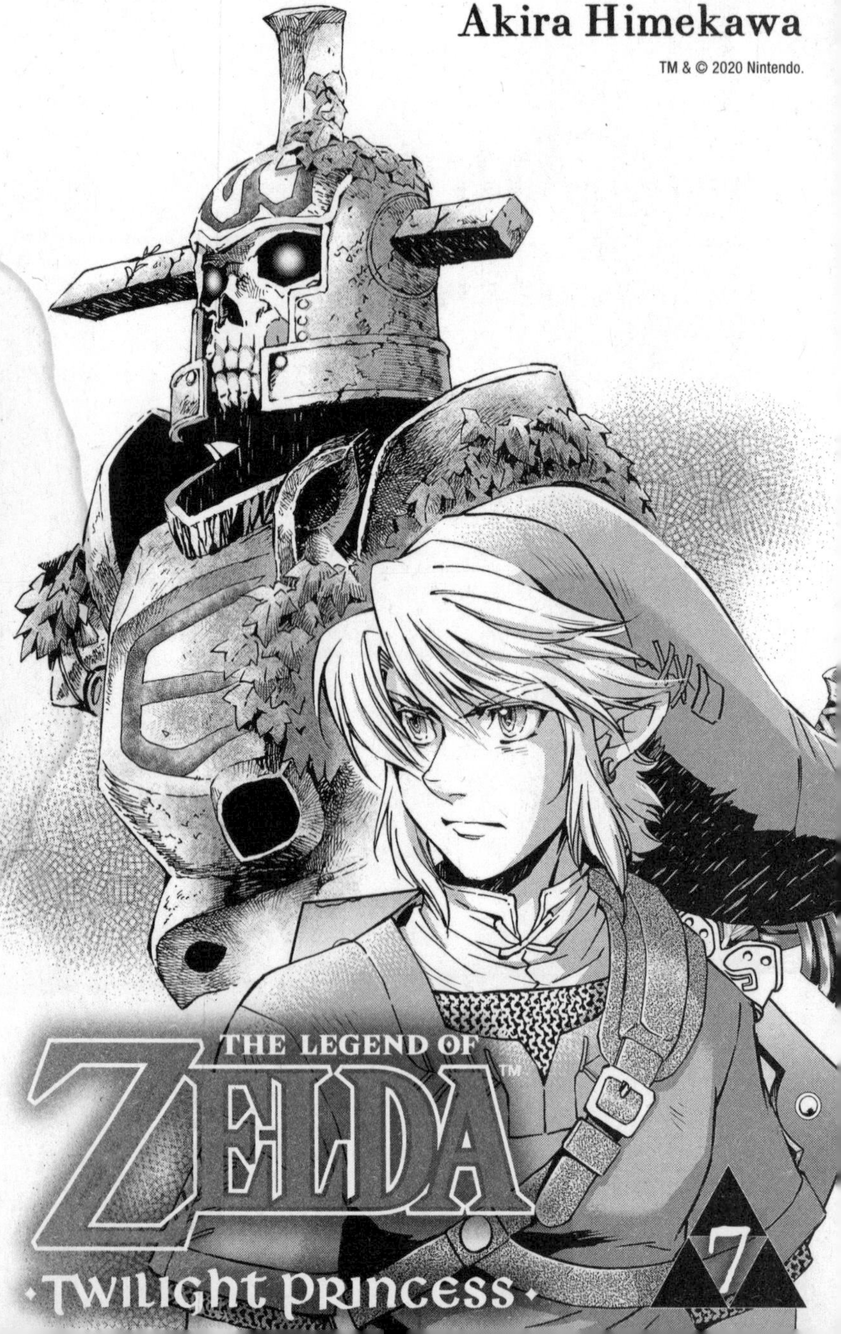